The Beast of Chicago

NBM ComicsLit

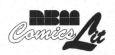

ISBN 13: 978-1-56163-365-4
©2003 Rick Geary

Third Printing

Library of Congress Cataloging-in-Publication Data

Geary, Rick.
   The Beast of Chicago / Rick Geary.
      p. cm.
   Includes bibliographical references.
   ISBN 1-56163-362-3 (hc) -- ISBN 1-56163-365-8 (pbk.)
   1. Mudgett, Herman W., 1861-1896--Fiction. I. Title.

PN6727.G4B43 2003
741.5'973--dc21

                                                      2003054016

Comicslit is an imprint
and trademark of

NANTIER · BEALL · MINOUSTCHINE
Publishing inc.
new york

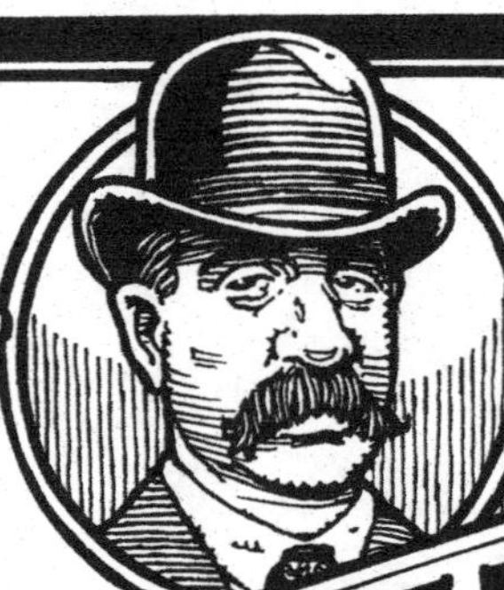

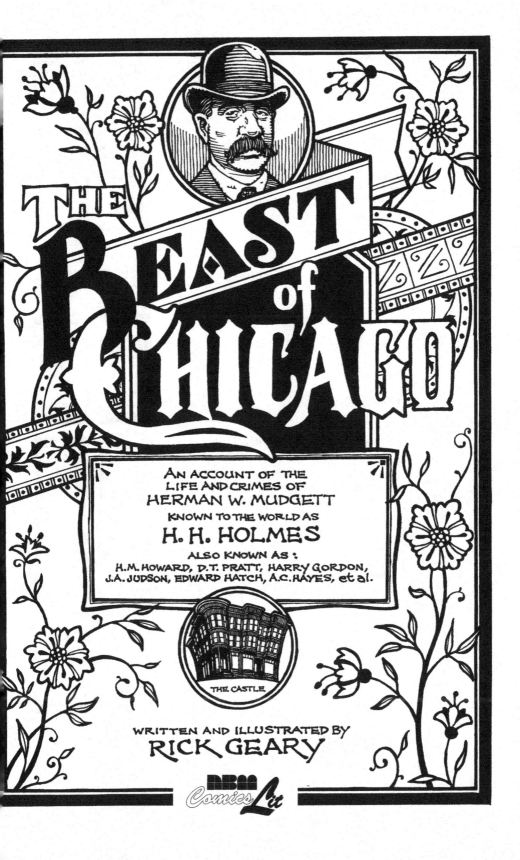

THE BEAST of CHICAGO

AN ACCOUNT OF THE
LIFE AND CRIMES OF
HERMAN W. MUDGETT
KNOWN TO THE WORLD AS
H. H. HOLMES
ALSO KNOWN AS :
H.M. HOWARD, D.T. PRATT, HARRY GORDON,
J.A. JUDSON, EDWARD HATCH, A.C. HAYES, et al.

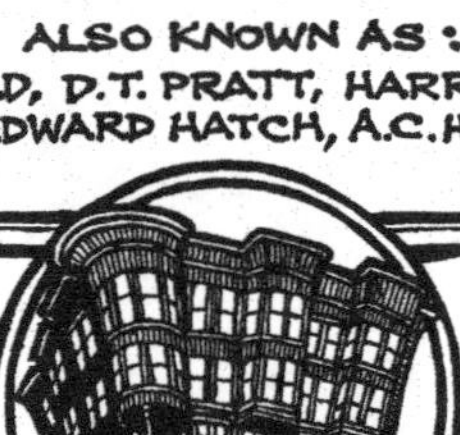
THE CASTLE

WRITTEN AND ILLUSTRATED BY
RICK GEARY

NBM ComicsLit

Also available by Geary:
A Treasury of Victorian Murder:
Vol. 1, pb.: $9.95, E-book: $6.99
Jack The Ripper pb.: $9.95
E-book: $6.99
The Borden Tragedy, pb.: $9.99
The Fatal Bullet, pb.: $9.95, E-book: $6.99
The Mystery of Mary Rogers
hc.: $15.95
The Beast of Chicago, E-book: $6.99
The Murder of Abraham Lincoln
pb.: $9.95, hc.: $15.95, E-book: $6.99
The Case of Madeleine Smith
pb.: $8.95, hc.: $15.95
The Bloody Benders
pb.: $9.95, E-book: $6.99
A Treasury of XXth Century Murder:
The Lindbergh Child
pb.: $9.95, hc.: $15.95, E-book: $6.99
Famous Players
pb.: $9.95, hc.: $15.95, , E-book: $6.99
The Axe-Man of New Orleans
hc.: $15.99, E-book: $6.99
The Lives of Sacco & Vanzetti
hc.: $15.99
Lovers Lane
hc.: $15.99, E-book: $6.99
The Lives of Sacco & Vanzetti
hc.: $15.99, E-book: $6.99
A Treasury of Victorian Murder Compendium
hc.: $24.99

See more on these
at our website:
www.nbmpublishing.com

P&H: $4 1st item, $1 each addt'l.

We have over 200 titles,
write for our color catalog:
NBM
160 Broadway, Suite 700, East Wing,
New York, NY 10038

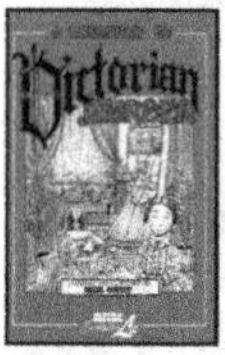
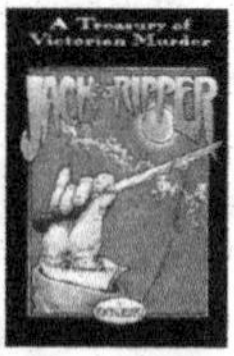
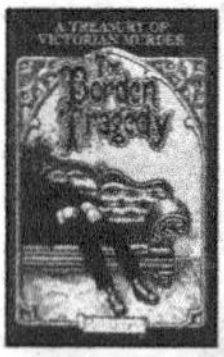
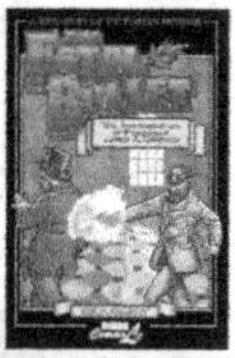
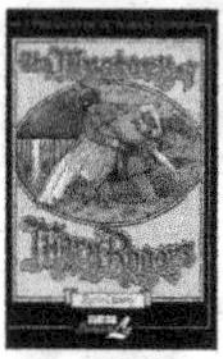
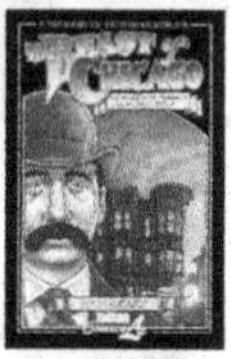
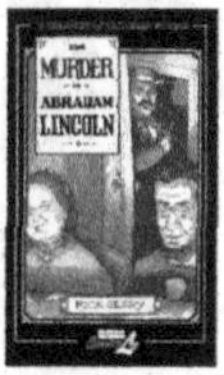
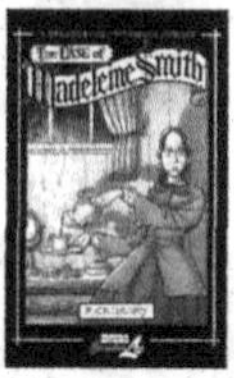
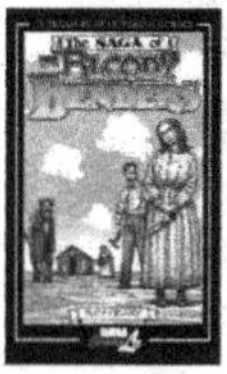
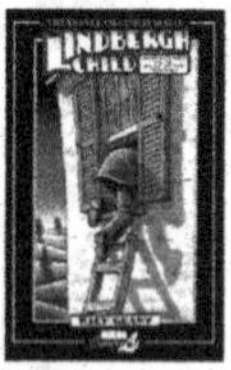
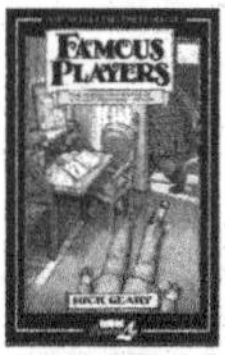
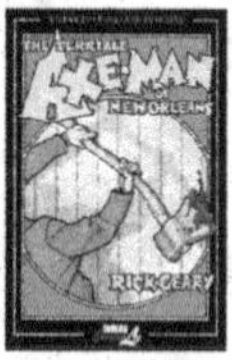
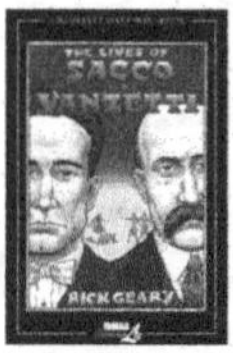
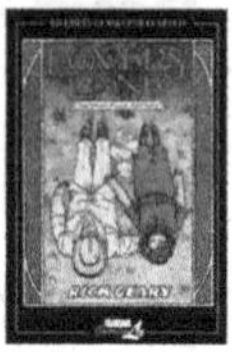
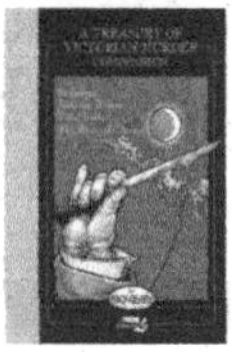

Comicslit is an imprint
and trademark of
NANTIER · BEALL · MINOUSTCHINE
Publishing inc.
new york

INTRODUCTION

"I couldn't help the fact that I was a murderer, no more than a poet can help the inspiration to sing."
H.H. Holmes

Only recently has the man known as H. H. Holmes achieved the status he deserves as 19th century America's preeminent monster. It is impossible to know today how many people he murdered. He confessed, at one time, to twenty-seven, but authoritative estimates placed the total at close to one hundred (while popular speculation boosted it to over twice that many). During Chicago's Columbian Exposition of 1893, his "Castle" in the suburb of Englewood did a thriving business as a rooming house to the visiting multitudes. For that crowded summer, it was also, in effect, a murder factory.

His capture and trial were covered thoroughly in the national press at the time, yet relatively little is known today of this man whose coldbloodedness has served as model for so many twentieth century killers. Holmes never passed into the national mythology-like Lizzie Borden, Billy the Kid and other legendary types- no doubt because what he did fell far outside any public understanding of human motivation.

Holmes is generally thought to be America's first serial killer. Rather, he was the first American to be caught and convicted for having committed multiple murders over a period of time. Surely others went before him whose crimes remain, as yet, unrecognized.

BIBLIOGRAPHY

Bloch, Robert, "Dr. Holmes's Murder Castle," reprinted in Readers Digest Tales of the Uncanny: True Stories of the Unexplained. (Pleasantville, New York, Readers Digest Assn., Inc, 1983)

Franke, David, The Torture Doctor. (New York, Hawthorne Books, Inc., 1975)

Lindberg, Richard, Chicago Ragtime. (South Bend, Indiana, Icarus Press, 1985)

Mayer, Harold M. and Richard C. Wade, Chicago, Growth of a Metropolis. (Chicago, University of Chicago Press, 1973)

Schechter, Harold, Depraved, the Shocking True Story of America's First Serial Killer. (New York, Pocket Books, 1994)

Seltzer, Mark, Serial Killers, Death and Life in America's Wound Culture. (New York, Rutledge, 1998)

Shaw, Marian, World's Fair Notes. (Pogo Press, 1992)

Swanson, Stevenson, Chicago Days, 150 Defining Moments in the Life of a Great City. (Chicago, Cantigny First Division Foundation, 1997)

Wilson, Colin, "H. H. Holmes, The Torture Doctor." The Mammoth Book of Murder, Richard Glyn Jones, ed. (New York, Carroll & Graf, 1989)

Special thanks to John Borowski

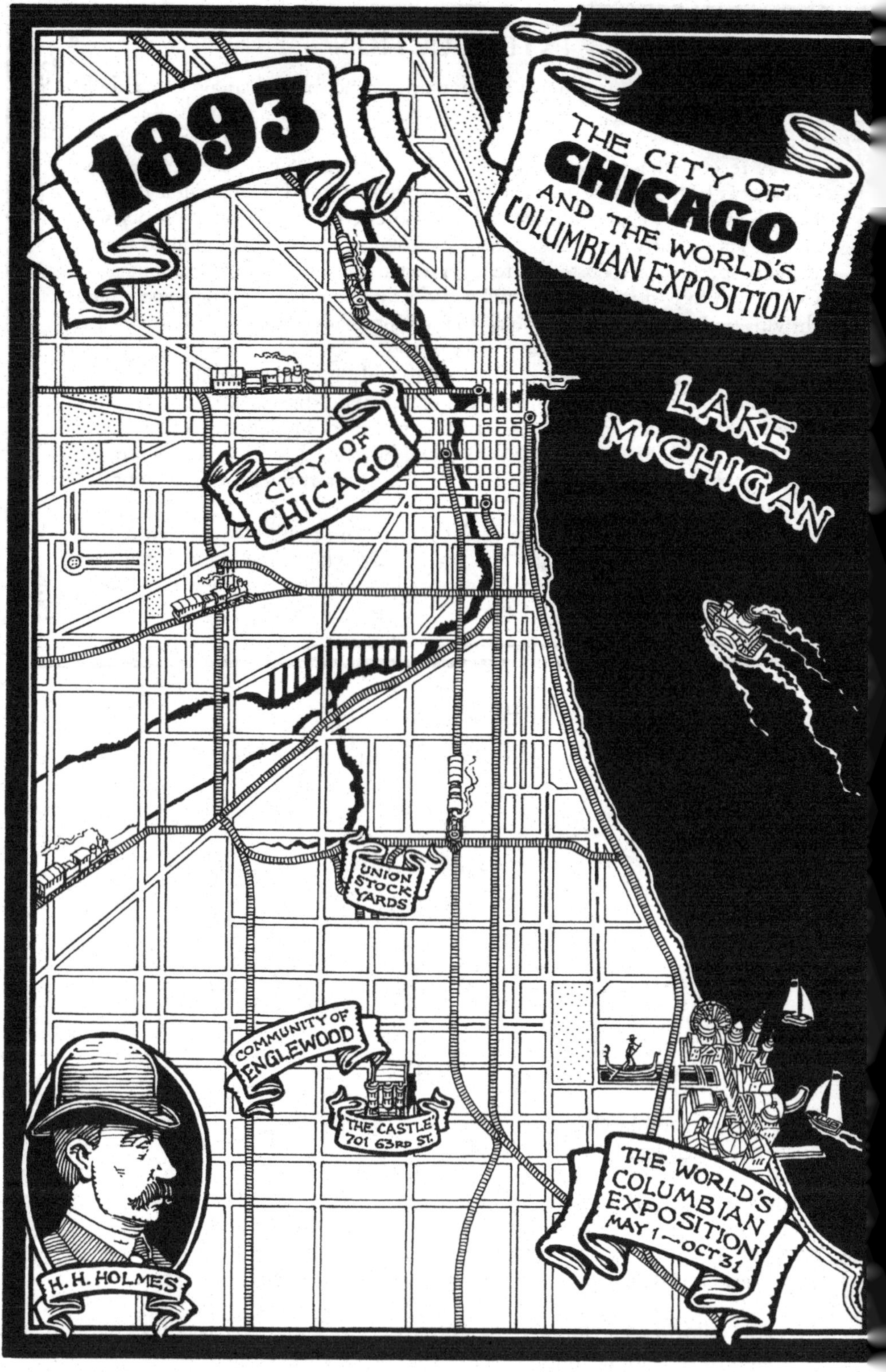
1893
THE CITY OF CHICAGO AND THE WORLD'S COLUMBIAN EXPOSITION
LAKE MICHIGAN
CITY OF CHICAGO
UNION STOCK YARDS
COMMUNITY OF ENGLEWOOD
THE CASTLE 701 63RD ST.
THE WORLD'S COLUMBIAN EXPOSITION MAY 1 ~ OCT 31
H. H. HOLMES

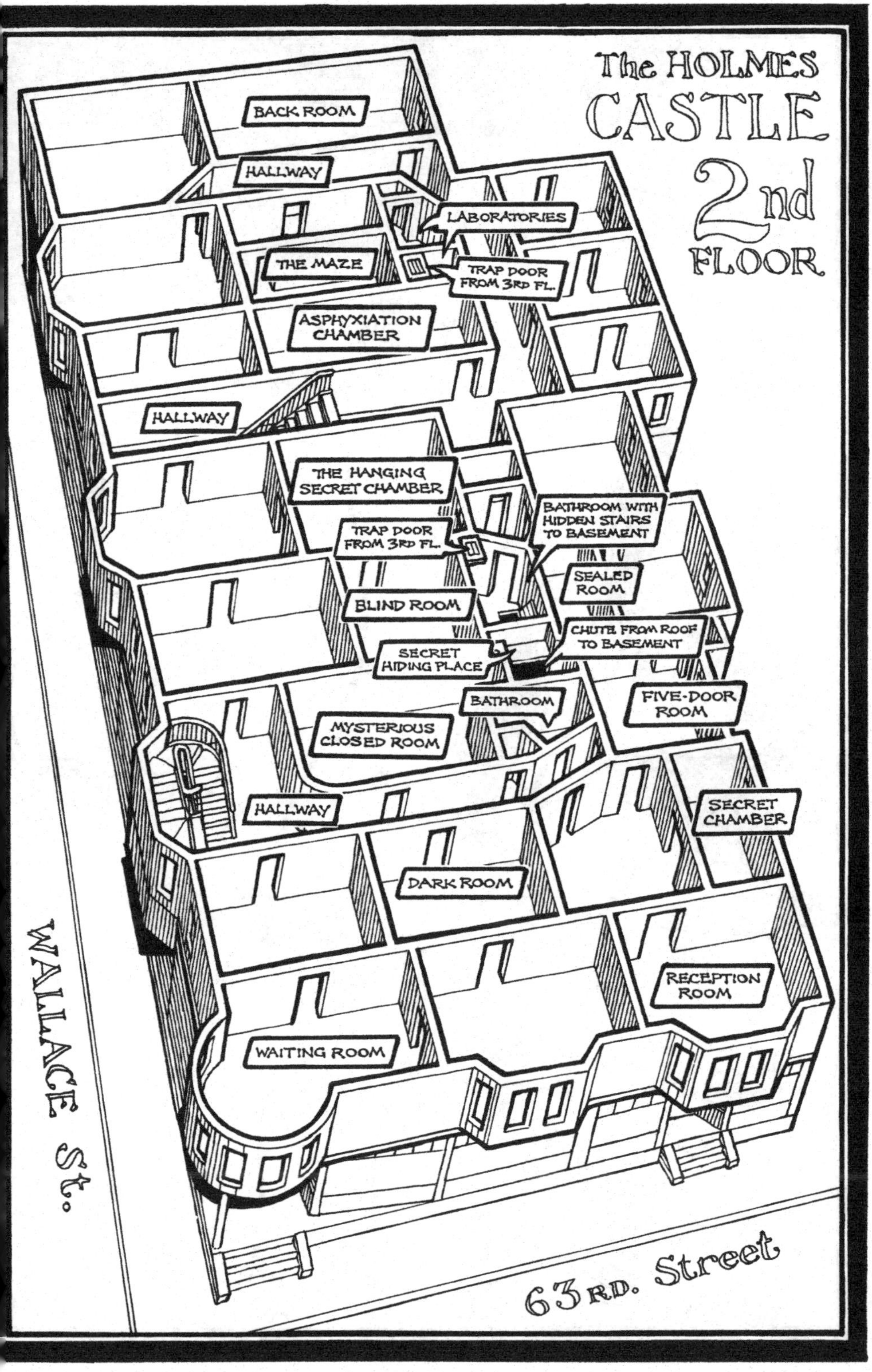
The HOLMES
CASTLE
2nd
FLOOR
BACK ROOM
HALLWAY
LABORATORIES
THE MAZE
TRAP DOOR FROM 3RD FL.
ASPHYXIATION CHAMBER
HALLWAY
THE HANGING SECRET CHAMBER
BATHROOM WITH HIDDEN STAIRS TO BASEMENT
TRAP DOOR FROM 3RD FL.
SEALED ROOM
BLIND ROOM
CHUTE FROM ROOF TO BASEMENT
SECRET HIDING PLACE
BATHROOM
FIVE-DOOR ROOM
MYSTERIOUS CLOSED ROOM
HALLWAY
SECRET CHAMBER
DARK ROOM
RECEPTION ROOM
WAITING ROOM
WALLACE St.
63RD. Street

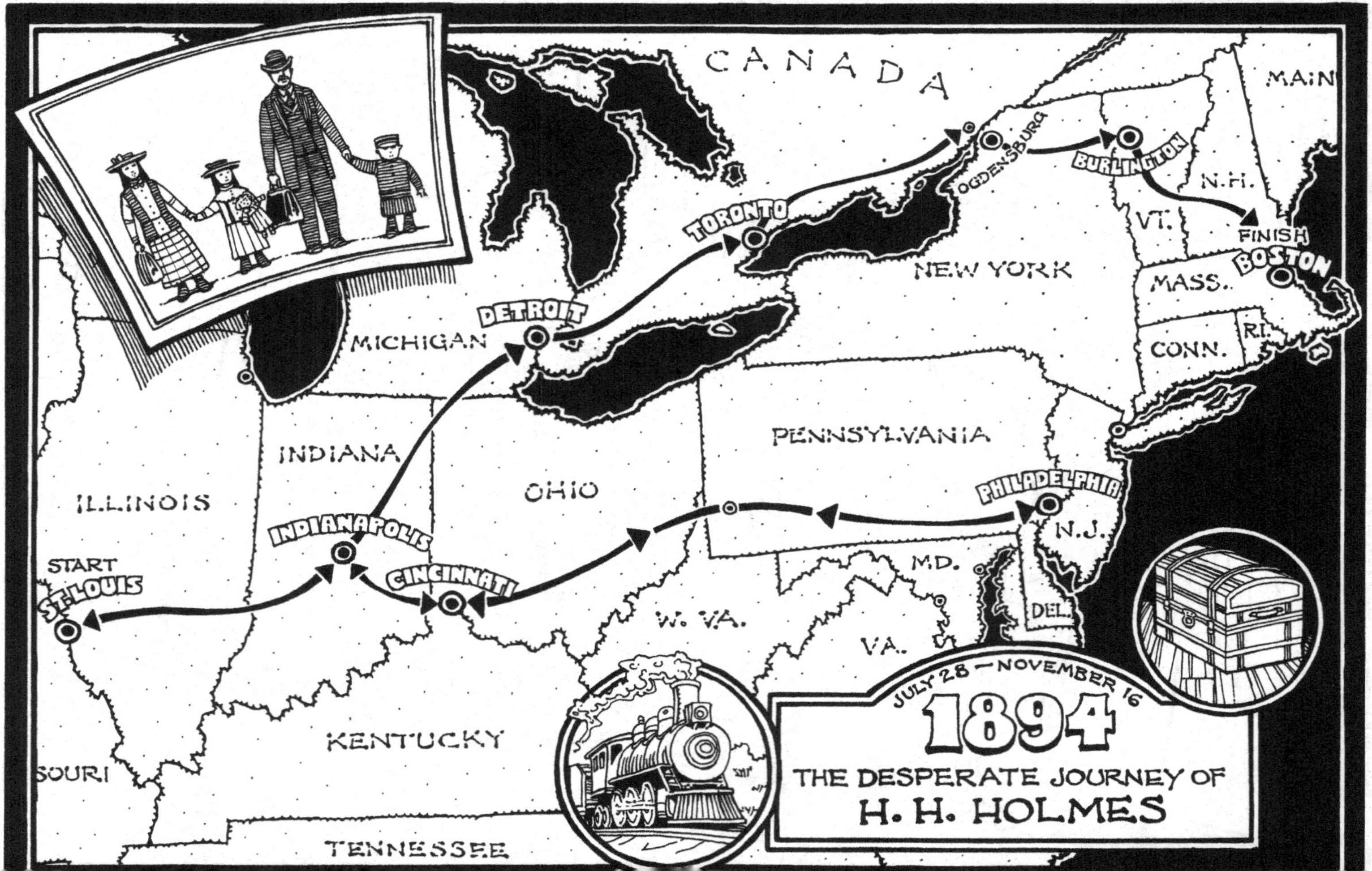

1894
JULY 28 — NOVEMBER 16
THE DESPERATE JOURNEY OF
H. H. HOLMES
CANADA
MAIN
N.H.
VT.
MASS.
R.I.
CONN.
NEW YORK
PENNSYLVANIA
N.J.
DEL.
MD.
VA.
W. VA.
OHIO
MICHIGAN
INDIANA
ILLINOIS
KENTUCKY
TENNESSEE
SOURI
START
ST. LOUIS
INDIANAPOLIS
CINCINNATI
DETROIT
TORONTO
OGDENSBURG
BURLINGTON
FINISH
BOSTON
PHILADELPHIA

PROLOGUE:
THIS IS CHICAGO!

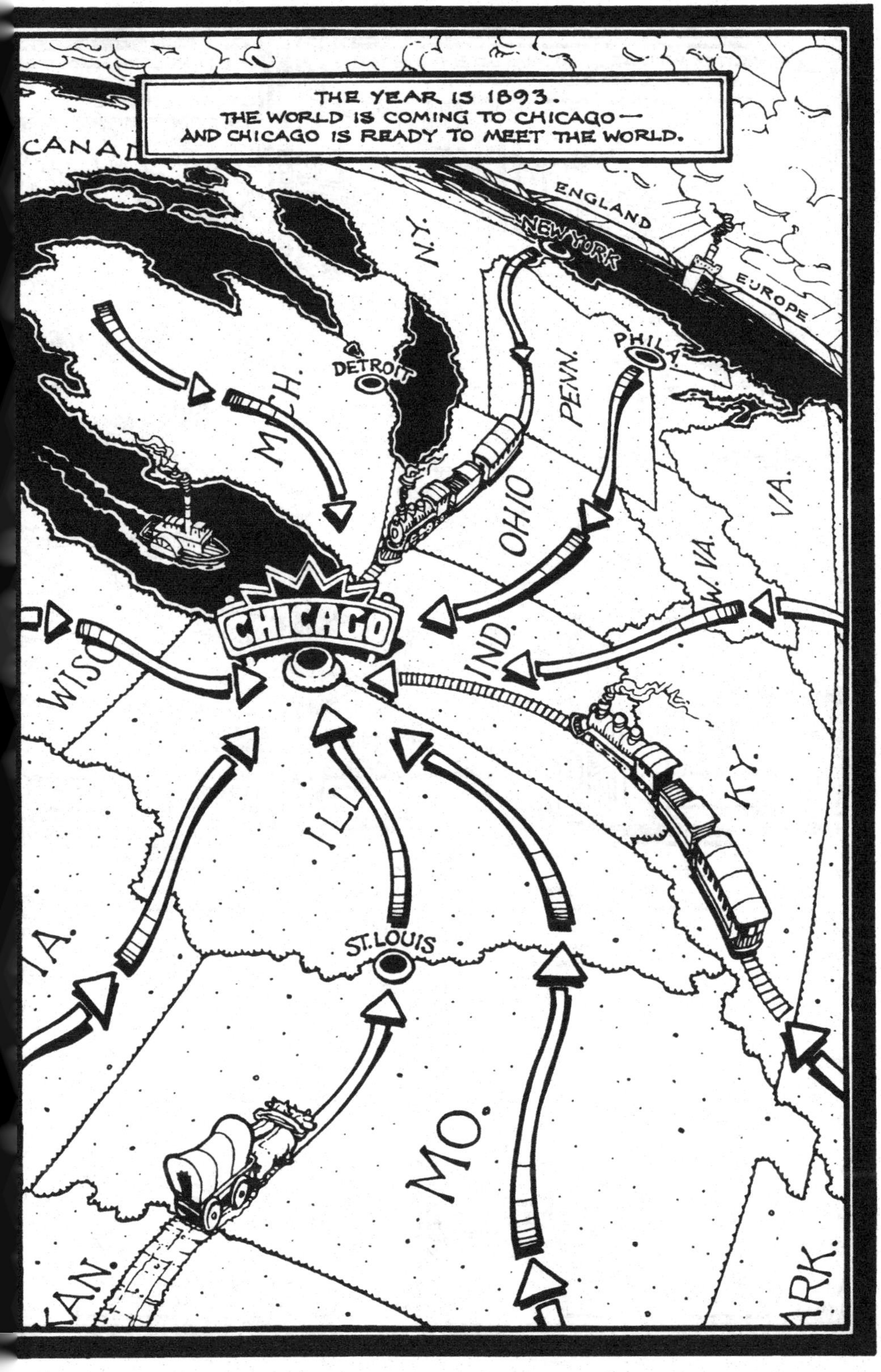
THE YEAR IS 1893.
THE WORLD IS COMING TO CHICAGO—
AND CHICAGO IS READY TO MEET THE WORLD.
CANAD
ENGLAND
NEW YORK
EUROPE
N.Y.
PHILA.
PENN.
DETROIT
MICH.
OHIO
VA.
W. VA.
CHICAGO
IND.
WISC
KY.
ILL.
IA.
ST. LOUIS
MO.
KAN.
ARK.

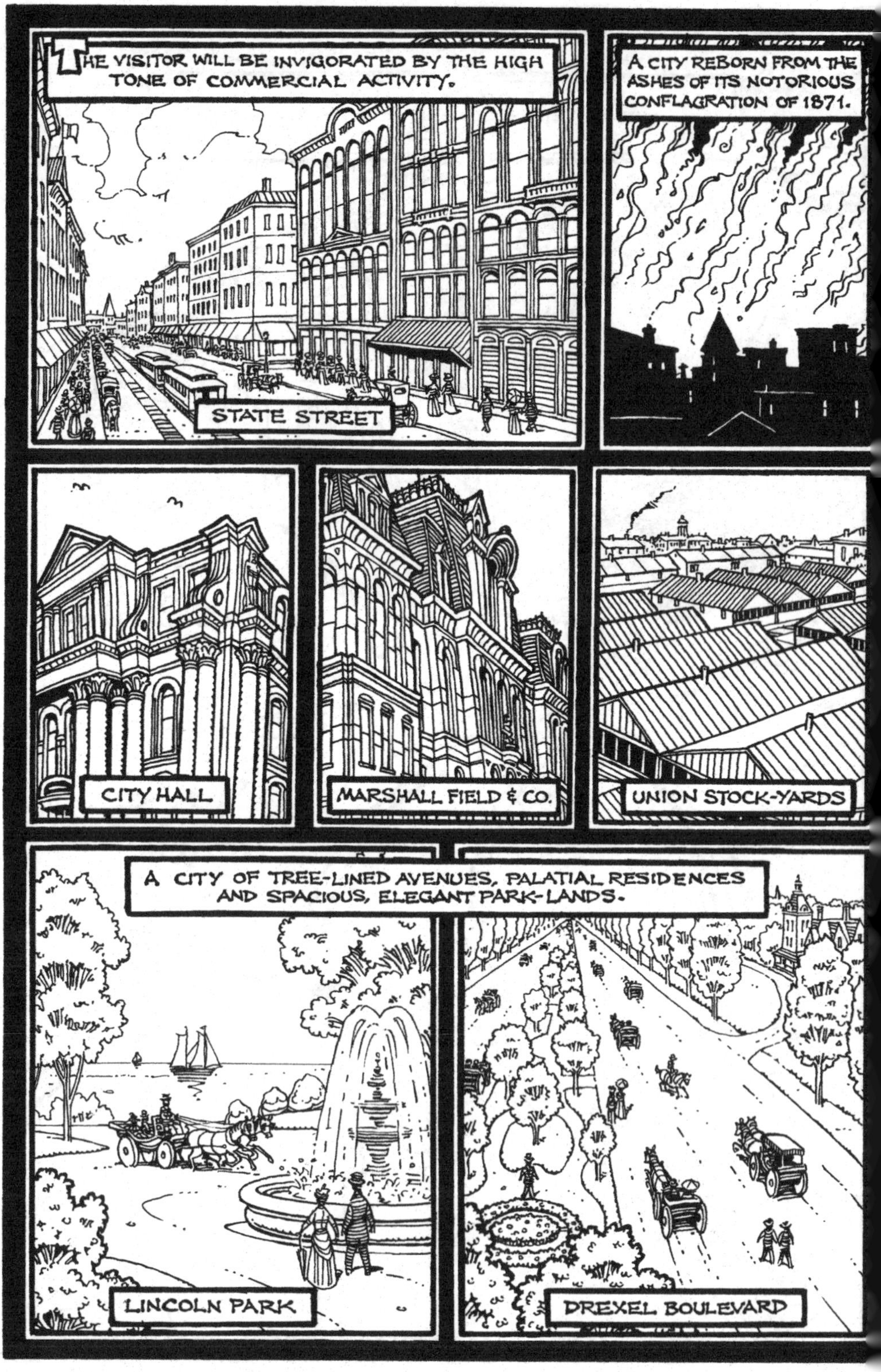
THE VISITOR WILL BE INVIGORATED BY THE HIGH TONE OF COMMERCIAL ACTIVITY.
STATE STREET
A CITY REBORN FROM THE ASHES OF ITS NOTORIOUS CONFLAGRATION OF 1871.
CITY HALL
MARSHALL FIELD & CO.
UNION STOCK-YARDS
A CITY OF TREE-LINED AVENUES, PALATIAL RESIDENCES AND SPACIOUS, ELEGANT PARK-LANDS.
LINCOLN PARK
DREXEL BOULEVARD

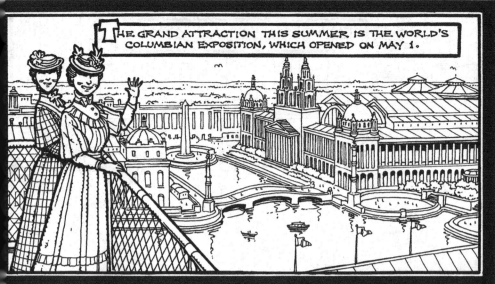
THE GRAND ATTRACTION THIS SUMMER IS THE WORLD'S COLUMBIAN EXPOSITION, WHICH OPENED ON MAY 1.

AGRICULTURAL HALL.

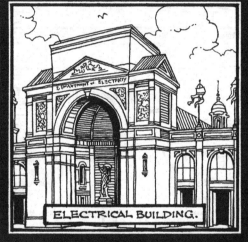
ELECTRICAL BUILDING.

BY DAY: "THE WHITE CITY."

BY NIGHT: "CITY OF LIGHT."

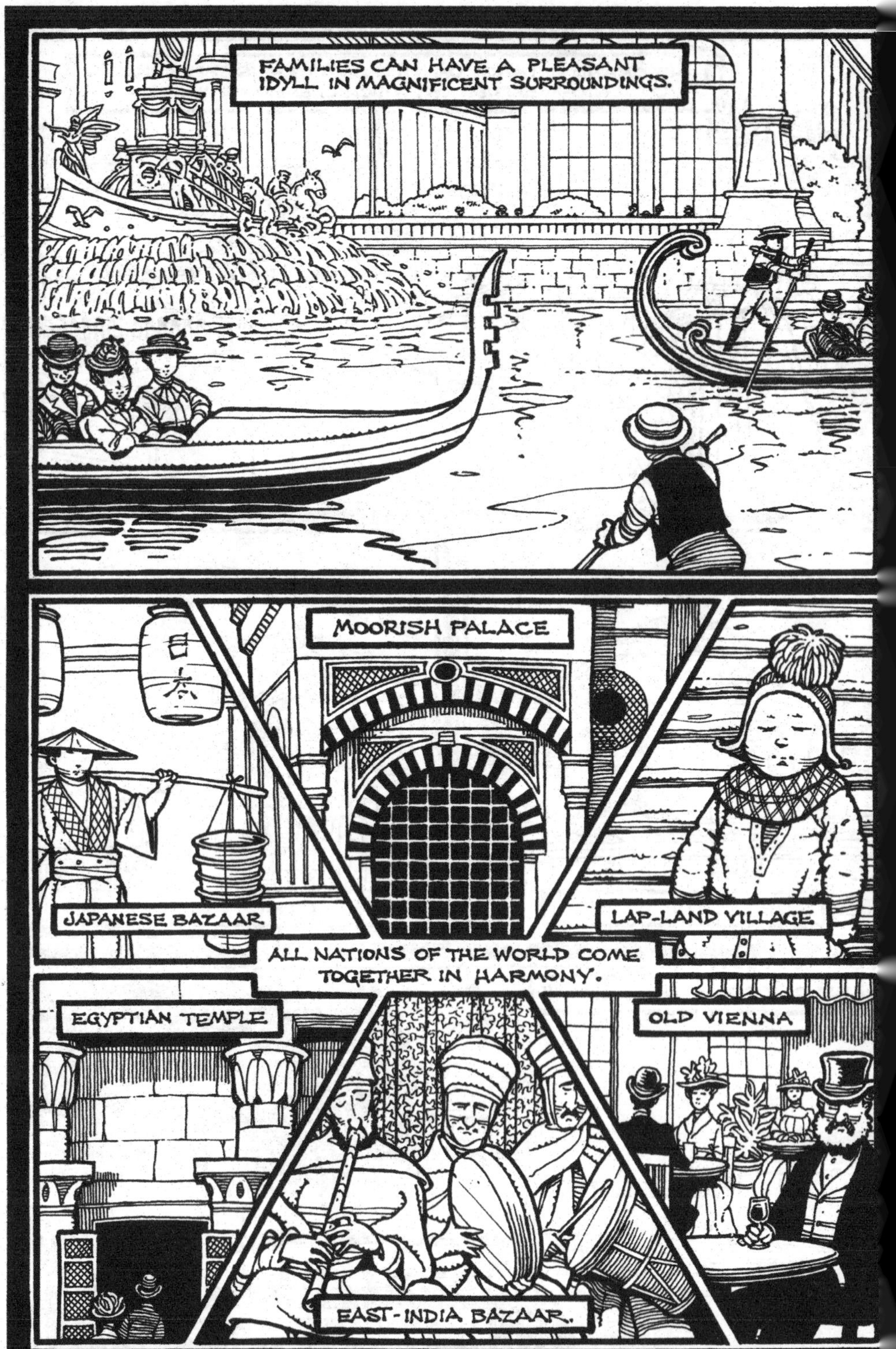
FAMILIES CAN HAVE A PLEASANT IDYLL IN MAGNIFICENT SURROUNDINGS.
MOORISH PALACE
JAPANESE BAZAAR
LAP-LAND VILLAGE
ALL NATIONS OF THE WORLD COME TOGETHER IN HARMONY.
EGYPTIAN TEMPLE
OLD VIENNA
EAST-INDIA BAZAAR.

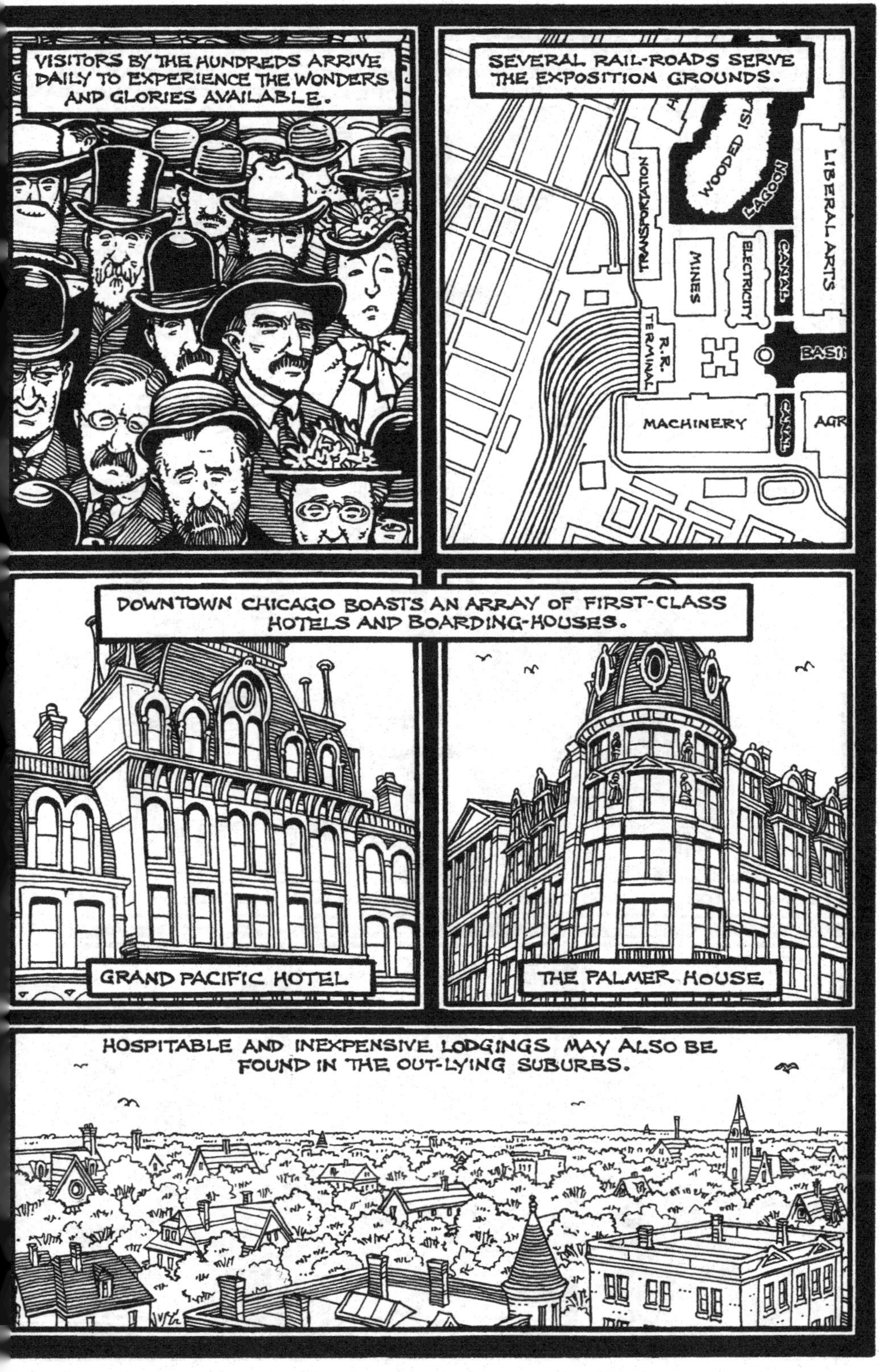
VISITORS BY THE HUNDREDS ARRIVE DAILY TO EXPERIENCE THE WONDERS AND GLORIES AVAILABLE.
SEVERAL RAIL-ROADS SERVE THE EXPOSITION GROUNDS.
TRANSPORTATION
LAGOON
LIBERAL ARTS
MINES
ELECTRICITY
CANAL
R.R. TERMINAL
MACHINERY
CANAL
DOWNTOWN CHICAGO BOASTS AN ARRAY OF FIRST-CLASS HOTELS AND BOARDING-HOUSES.
GRAND PACIFIC HOTEL
THE PALMER HOUSE
HOSPITABLE AND INEXPENSIVE LODGINGS MAY ALSO BE FOUND IN THE OUT-LYING SUBURBS.

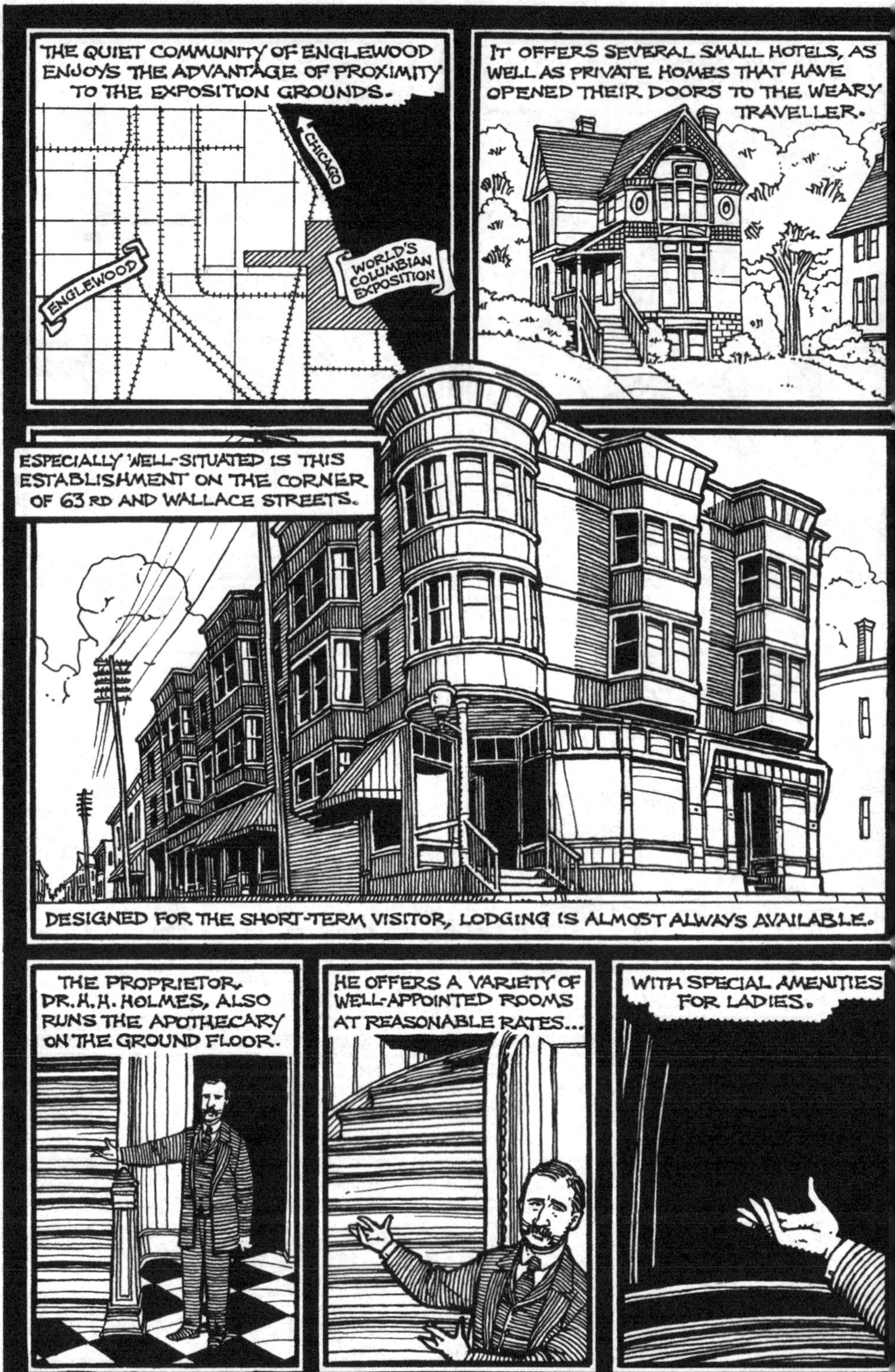
THE QUIET COMMUNITY OF ENGLEWOOD ENJOYS THE ADVANTAGE OF PROXIMITY TO THE EXPOSITION GROUNDS.
CHICAGO
ENGLEWOOD
WORLD'S COLUMBIAN EXPOSITION
IT OFFERS SEVERAL SMALL HOTELS, AS WELL AS PRIVATE HOMES THAT HAVE OPENED THEIR DOORS TO THE WEARY TRAVELLER.
ESPECIALLY WELL-SITUATED IS THIS ESTABLISHMENT ON THE CORNER OF 63 RD AND WALLACE STREETS.
DESIGNED FOR THE SHORT-TERM VISITOR, LODGING IS ALMOST ALWAYS AVAILABLE.
THE PROPRIETOR, DR. H. H. HOLMES, ALSO RUNS THE APOTHECARY ON THE GROUND FLOOR.
HE OFFERS A VARIETY OF WELL-APPOINTED ROOMS AT REASONABLE RATES...
WITH SPECIAL AMENITIES FOR LADIES.

PART I.

DR. HOLMES
COMES TO TOWN

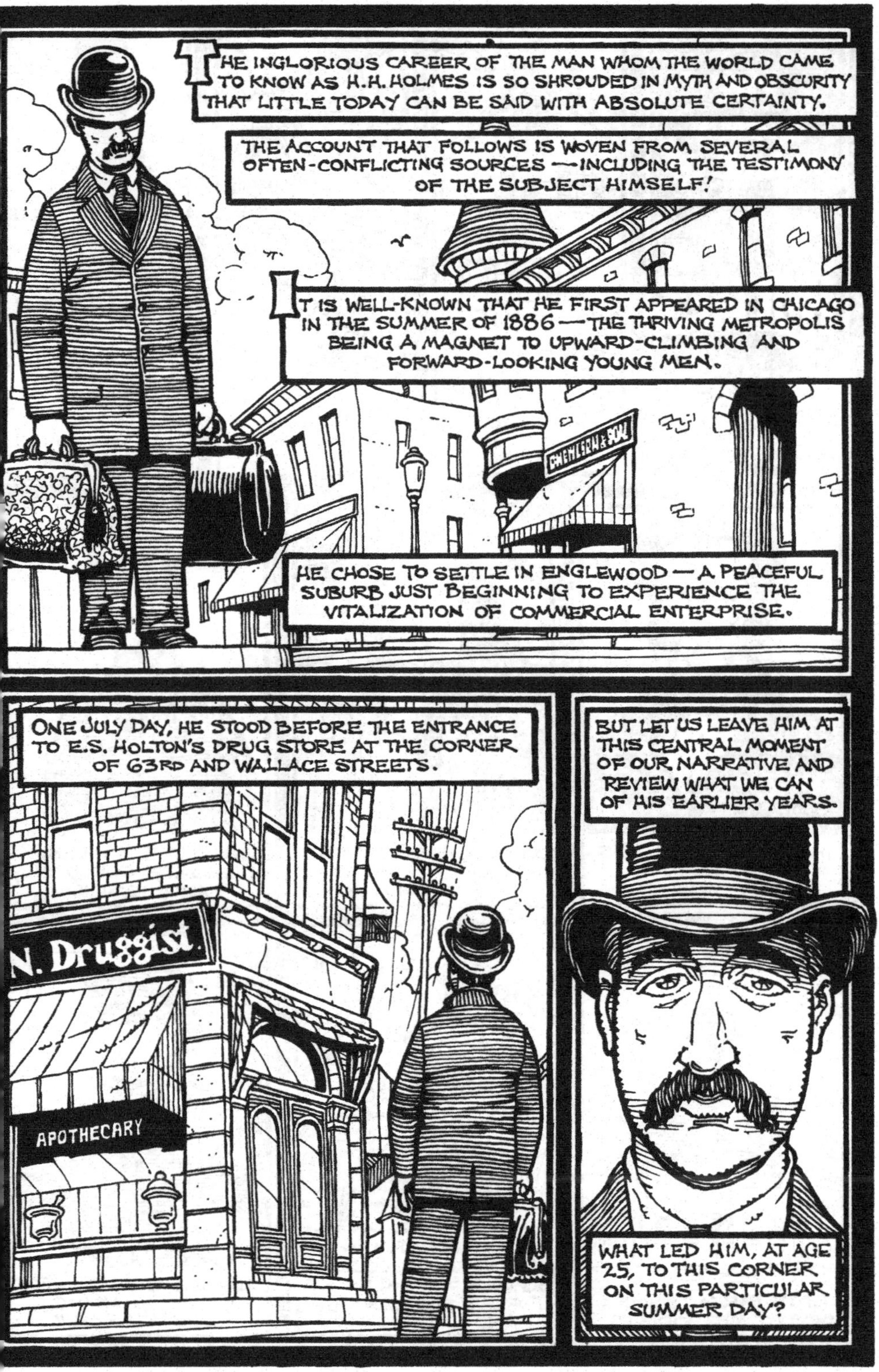
THE INGLORIOUS CAREER OF THE MAN WHOM THE WORLD CAME TO KNOW AS H.H. HOLMES IS SO SHROUDED IN MYTH AND OBSCURITY THAT LITTLE TODAY CAN BE SAID WITH ABSOLUTE CERTAINTY.
THE ACCOUNT THAT FOLLOWS IS WOVEN FROM SEVERAL OFTEN-CONFLICTING SOURCES — INCLUDING THE TESTIMONY OF THE SUBJECT HIMSELF!
IT IS WELL-KNOWN THAT HE FIRST APPEARED IN CHICAGO IN THE SUMMER OF 1886 — THE THRIVING METROPOLIS BEING A MAGNET TO UPWARD-CLIMBING AND FORWARD-LOOKING YOUNG MEN.
HE CHOSE TO SETTLE IN ENGLEWOOD — A PEACEFUL SUBURB JUST BEGINNING TO EXPERIENCE THE VITALIZATION OF COMMERCIAL ENTERPRISE.
ONE JULY DAY, HE STOOD BEFORE THE ENTRANCE TO E.S. HOLTON'S DRUG STORE AT THE CORNER OF 63RD AND WALLACE STREETS.
N. Druggist.
APOTHECARY
BUT LET US LEAVE HIM AT THIS CENTRAL MOMENT OF OUR NARRATIVE AND REVIEW WHAT WE CAN OF HIS EARLIER YEARS.
WHAT LED HIM, AT AGE 25, TO THIS CORNER ON THIS PARTICULAR SUMMER DAY?

THE EARLY YEARS OF H.H. HOLMES

WE NOW KNOW THAT HE WAS BORN HERMAN WEBSTER MUDGETT ON MAY 16, 1861...

IN THE TOWN OF GILMANTON...

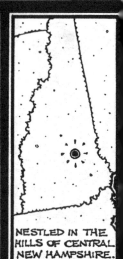

NESTLED IN THE HILLS OF CENTRAL NEW HAMPSHIRE.

THE FATHER, LEVI, WAS A FARMER AND POST-MASTER.

REPORTEDLY A HEAVY DRINKER, HE USED THE ROD LIBERALLY UPON HIS THREE OFFSPRING...

WHILE THE MOTHER, THEODATE, COULD ONLY ACQUIESCE.

BOTH PARENTS WERE DEVOUT METHODISTS.

YOUNG HERMAN ATTENDED THE LOCAL SCHOOLS, EARNING NOTICE FOR HIS SCHOLARSHIP AND AMBITION...

ALSO A REPUTATION FOR "OVER-BEARING ARROGANCE."

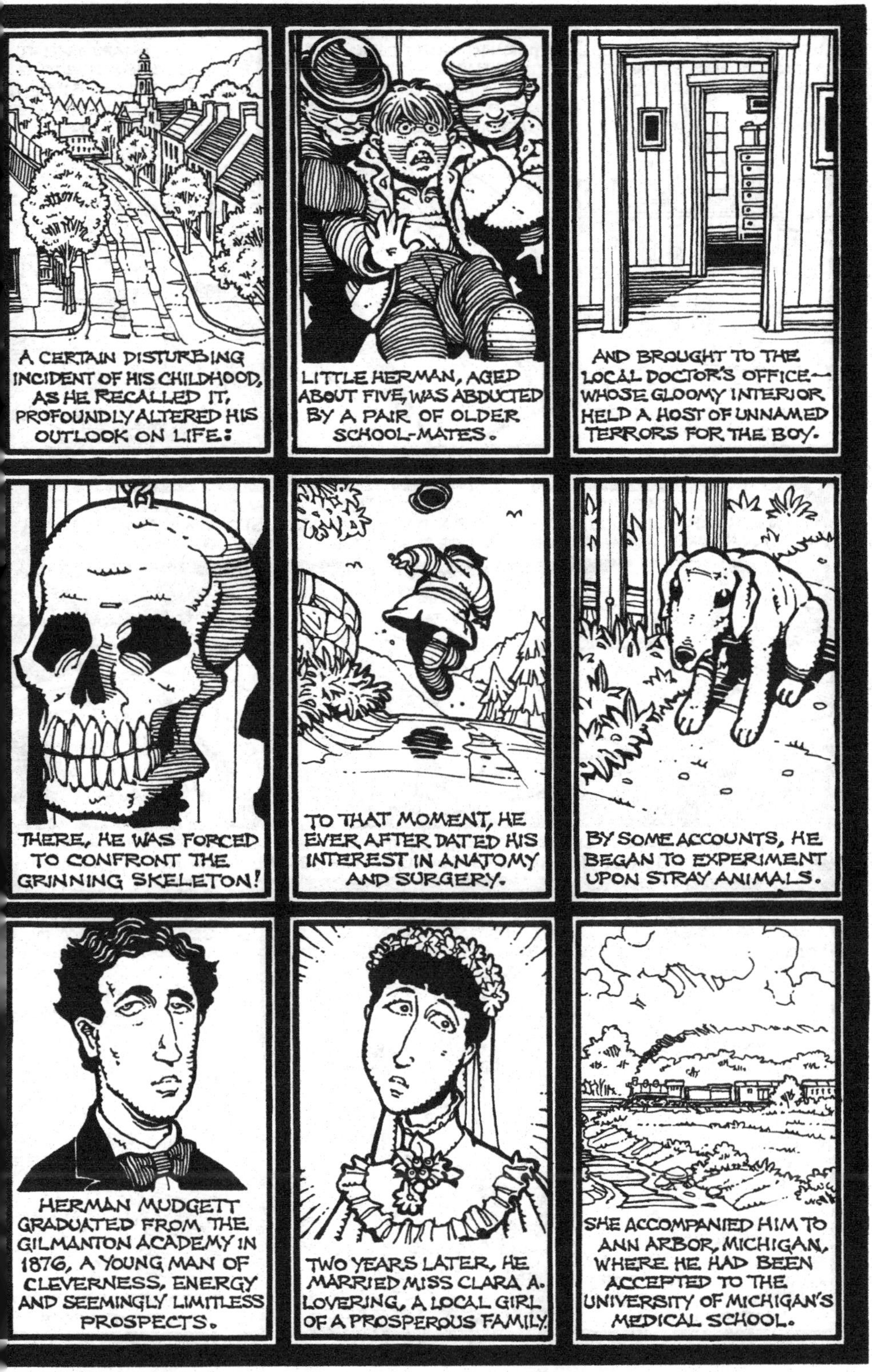
A CERTAIN DISTURBING INCIDENT OF HIS CHILDHOOD, AS HE RECALLED IT, PROFOUNDLY ALTERED HIS OUTLOOK ON LIFE:
LITTLE HERMAN, AGED ABOUT FIVE, WAS ABDUCTED BY A PAIR OF OLDER SCHOOL-MATES.
AND BROUGHT TO THE LOCAL DOCTOR'S OFFICE— WHOSE GLOOMY INTERIOR HELD A HOST OF UNNAMED TERRORS FOR THE BOY.
THERE, HE WAS FORCED TO CONFRONT THE GRINNING SKELETON!
TO THAT MOMENT, HE EVER AFTER DATED HIS INTEREST IN ANATOMY AND SURGERY.
BY SOME ACCOUNTS, HE BEGAN TO EXPERIMENT UPON STRAY ANIMALS.
HERMAN MUDGETT GRADUATED FROM THE GILMANTON ACADEMY IN 1876, A YOUNG MAN OF CLEVERNESS, ENERGY AND SEEMINGLY LIMITLESS PROSPECTS.
TWO YEARS LATER, HE MARRIED MISS CLARA A. LOVERING, A LOCAL GIRL OF A PROSPEROUS FAMILY.
SHE ACCOMPANIED HIM TO ANN ARBOR, MICHIGAN, WHERE HE HAD BEEN ACCEPTED TO THE UNIVERSITY OF MICHIGAN'S MEDICAL SCHOOL.

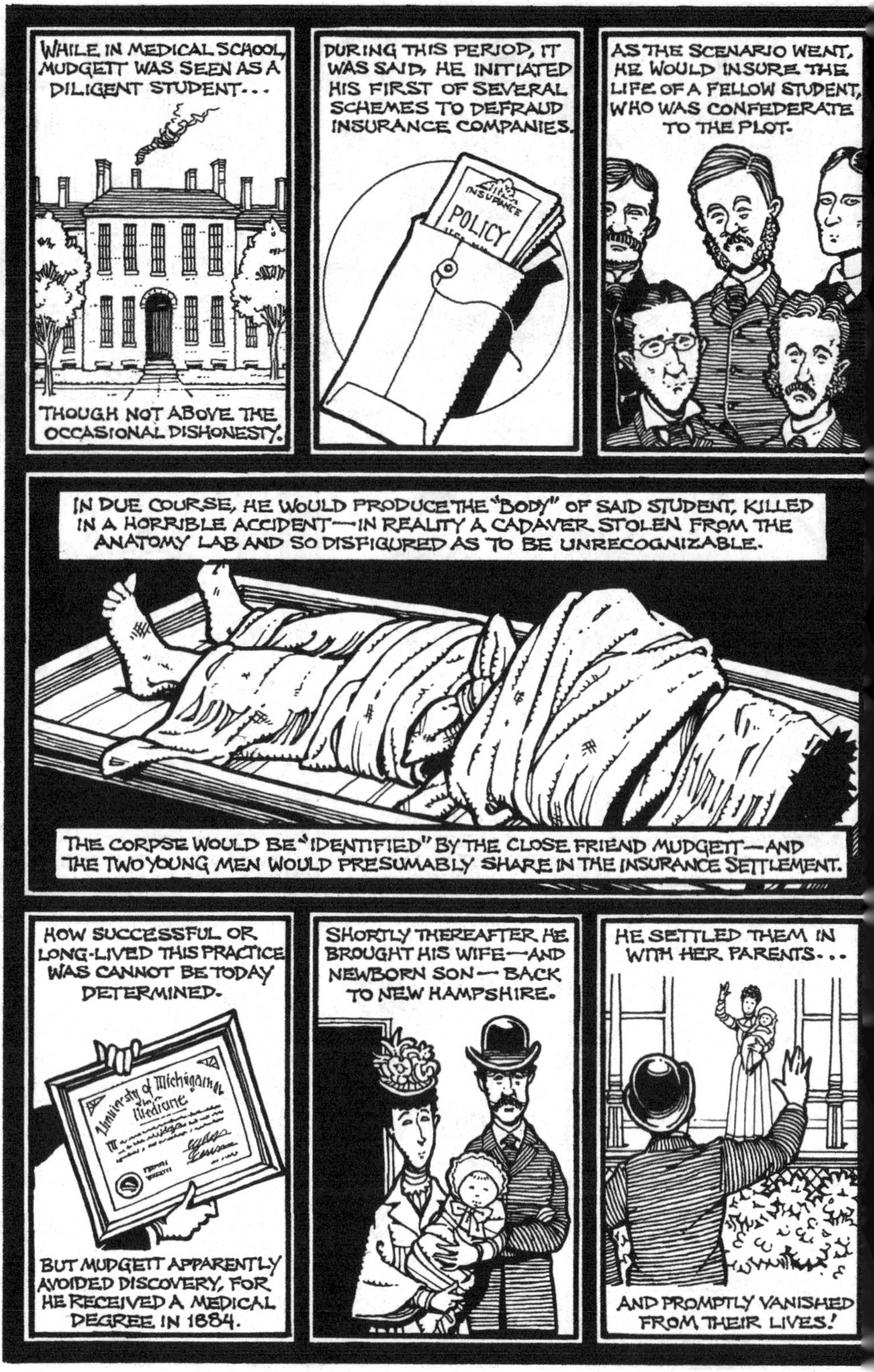
WHILE IN MEDICAL SCHOOL, MUDGETT WAS SEEN AS A DILIGENT STUDENT...
THOUGH NOT ABOVE THE OCCASIONAL DISHONESTY.
DURING THIS PERIOD, IT WAS SAID, HE INITIATED HIS FIRST OF SEVERAL SCHEMES TO DEFRAUD INSURANCE COMPANIES.
INSURANCE
POLICY
AS THE SCENARIO WENT, HE WOULD INSURE THE LIFE OF A FELLOW STUDENT, WHO WAS CONFEDERATE TO THE PLOT.
IN DUE COURSE, HE WOULD PRODUCE THE "BODY" OF SAID STUDENT, KILLED IN A HORRIBLE ACCIDENT—IN REALITY A CADAVER STOLEN FROM THE ANATOMY LAB AND SO DISFIGURED AS TO BE UNRECOGNIZABLE.
THE CORPSE WOULD BE "IDENTIFIED" BY THE CLOSE FRIEND MUDGETT—AND THE TWO YOUNG MEN WOULD PRESUMABLY SHARE IN THE INSURANCE SETTLEMENT.
HOW SUCCESSFUL OR LONG-LIVED THIS PRACTICE WAS CANNOT BE TODAY DETERMINED.
University of Michigan
Medicine
BUT MUDGETT APPARENTLY AVOIDED DISCOVERY, FOR HE RECEIVED A MEDICAL DEGREE IN 1884.
SHORTLY THEREAFTER HE BROUGHT HIS WIFE—AND NEWBORN SON—BACK TO NEW HAMPSHIRE.
HE SETTLED THEM IN WITH HER PARENTS...
AND PROMPTLY VANISHED FROM THEIR LIVES!

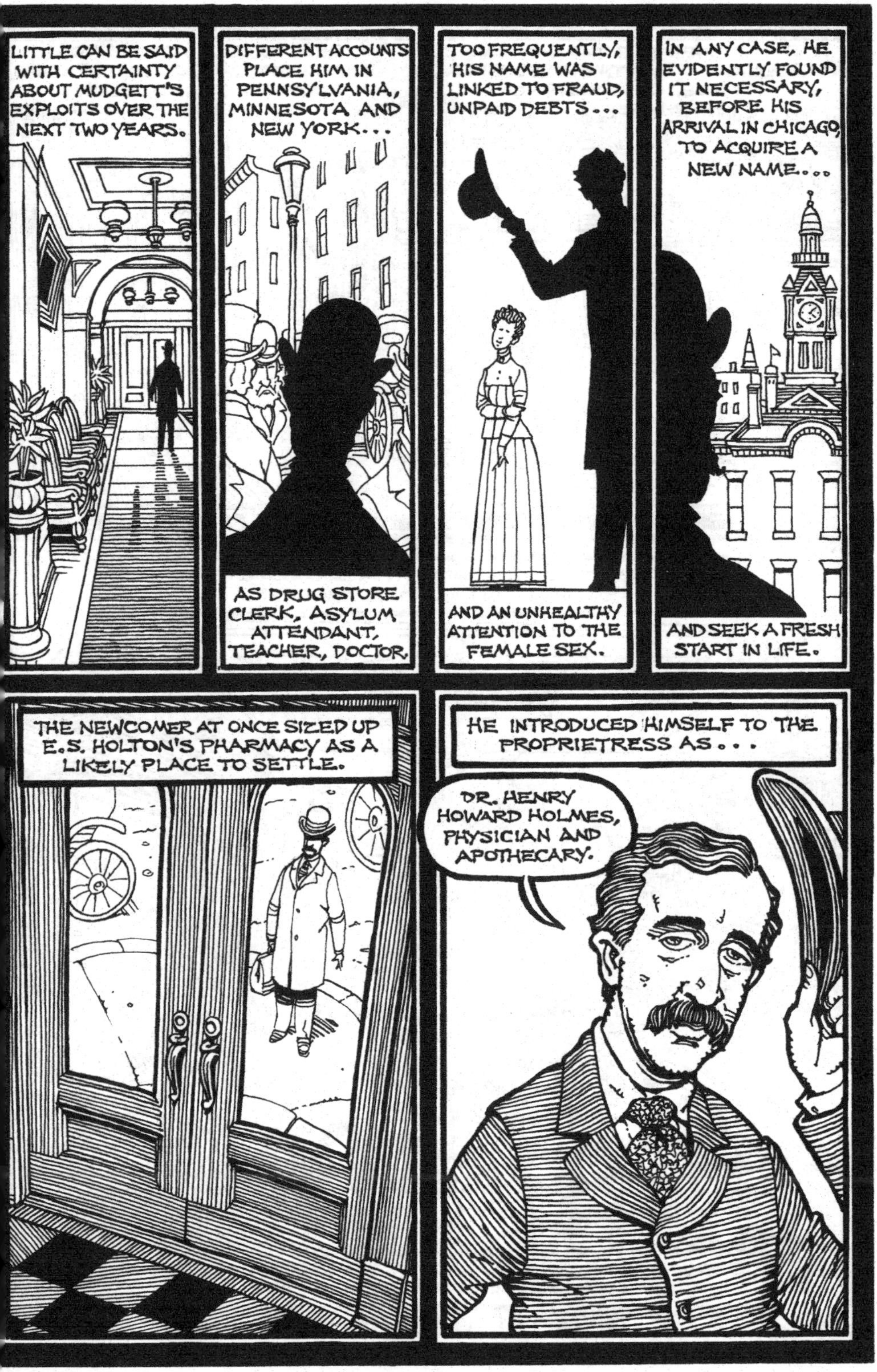
LITTLE CAN BE SAID WITH CERTAINTY ABOUT MUDGETT'S EXPLOITS OVER THE NEXT TWO YEARS.
DIFFERENT ACCOUNTS PLACE HIM IN PENNSYLVANIA, MINNESOTA AND NEW YORK...
AS DRUG STORE CLERK, ASYLUM ATTENDANT, TEACHER, DOCTOR.
TOO FREQUENTLY, HIS NAME WAS LINKED TO FRAUD, UNPAID DEBTS...
AND AN UNHEALTHY ATTENTION TO THE FEMALE SEX.
IN ANY CASE, HE EVIDENTLY FOUND IT NECESSARY, BEFORE HIS ARRIVAL IN CHICAGO, TO ACQUIRE A NEW NAME...
AND SEEK A FRESH START IN LIFE.
THE NEWCOMER AT ONCE SIZED UP E.S. HOLTON'S PHARMACY AS A LIKELY PLACE TO SETTLE.
HE INTRODUCED HIMSELF TO THE PROPRIETRESS AS...
DR. HENRY HOWARD HOLMES, PHYSICIAN AND APOTHECARY.

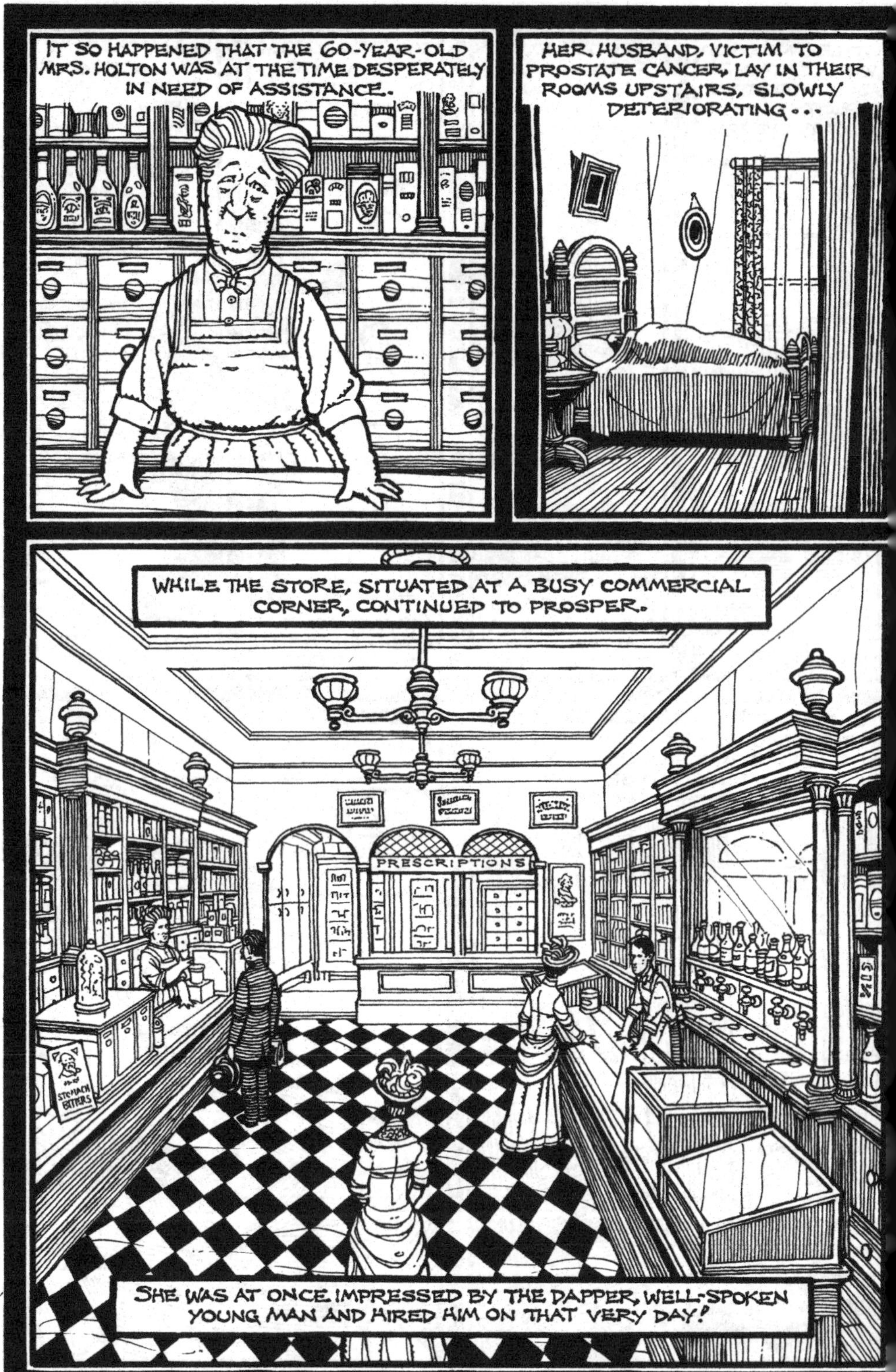
IT SO HAPPENED THAT THE 60-YEAR-OLD MRS. HOLTON WAS AT THE TIME DESPERATELY IN NEED OF ASSISTANCE.
HER HUSBAND, VICTIM TO PROSTATE CANCER, LAY IN THEIR ROOMS UPSTAIRS, SLOWLY DETERIORATING...
WHILE THE STORE, SITUATED AT A BUSY COMMERCIAL CORNER, CONTINUED TO PROSPER.
PRESCRIPTIONS
STOMACH BITTERS
SHE WAS AT ONCE IMPRESSED BY THE DAPPER, WELL-SPOKEN YOUNG MAN AND HIRED HIM ON THAT VERY DAY!

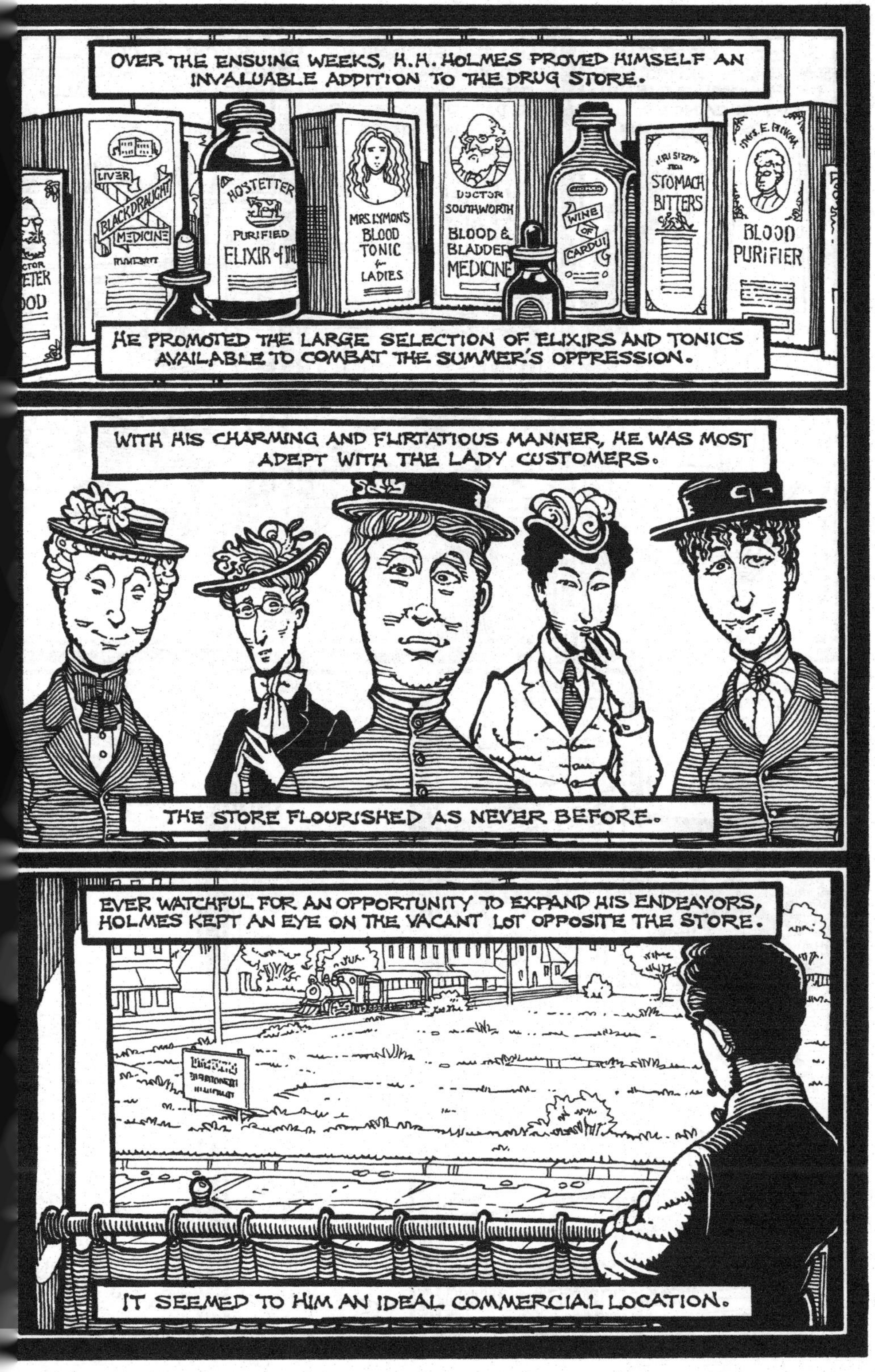
OVER THE ENSUING WEEKS, H.H. HOLMES PROVED HIMSELF AN INVALUABLE ADDITION TO THE DRUG STORE.
LIVER BLACKDRAUGHT MEDICINE
HOSTETTER PURIFIED ELIXIR
MRS. LYMON'S BLOOD TONIC for LADIES
DOCTOR SOUTHWORTH BLOOD & BLADDER MEDICINE
WINE OF CARDUI
STOMACH BITTERS
MRS. E. PINKHAM BLOOD PURIFIER
HE PROMOTED THE LARGE SELECTION OF ELIXIRS AND TONICS AVAILABLE TO COMBAT THE SUMMER'S OPPRESSION.
WITH HIS CHARMING AND FLIRTATIOUS MANNER, HE WAS MOST ADEPT WITH THE LADY CUSTOMERS.
THE STORE FLOURISHED AS NEVER BEFORE.
EVER WATCHFUL FOR AN OPPORTUNITY TO EXPAND HIS ENDEAVORS, HOLMES KEPT AN EYE ON THE VACANT LOT OPPOSITE THE STORE.
IT SEEMED TO HIM AN IDEAL COMMERCIAL LOCATION.

SOMETIME LATER THAT SUMMER, THE UNFORTUNATE DR. HOLTON PERISHED OF HIS CANCER

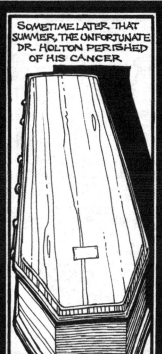

AND THE SORROWING WIDOW GRADUALLY WITHDREW HERSELF FROM THE DAY-TO-DAY OPERATION OF THE STORE . . .

LEAVING IN COMPLETE CHARGE THE HONEST AND CAPABLE DR. HOLMES.

IN SHORT ORDER, HE APPROACHED MRS. HOLTON WITH AN OFFER TO BUY THE ESTABLISHMENT. SHE READILY ACCEPTED.

BUT BEFORE THE YEAR WAS OUT, WITH NO PAYMENT FORTHCOMING, SHE INITIATED A LAWSUIT.

NOT LONG THEREAFTER, SHE VANISHED WITHOUT A TRACE.

TO ANY WHO INQUIRED, THE GOOD DOCTOR EXPLAINED THAT SHE HAD GONE TO LIVE WITH RELATIONS IN CALIFORNIA.

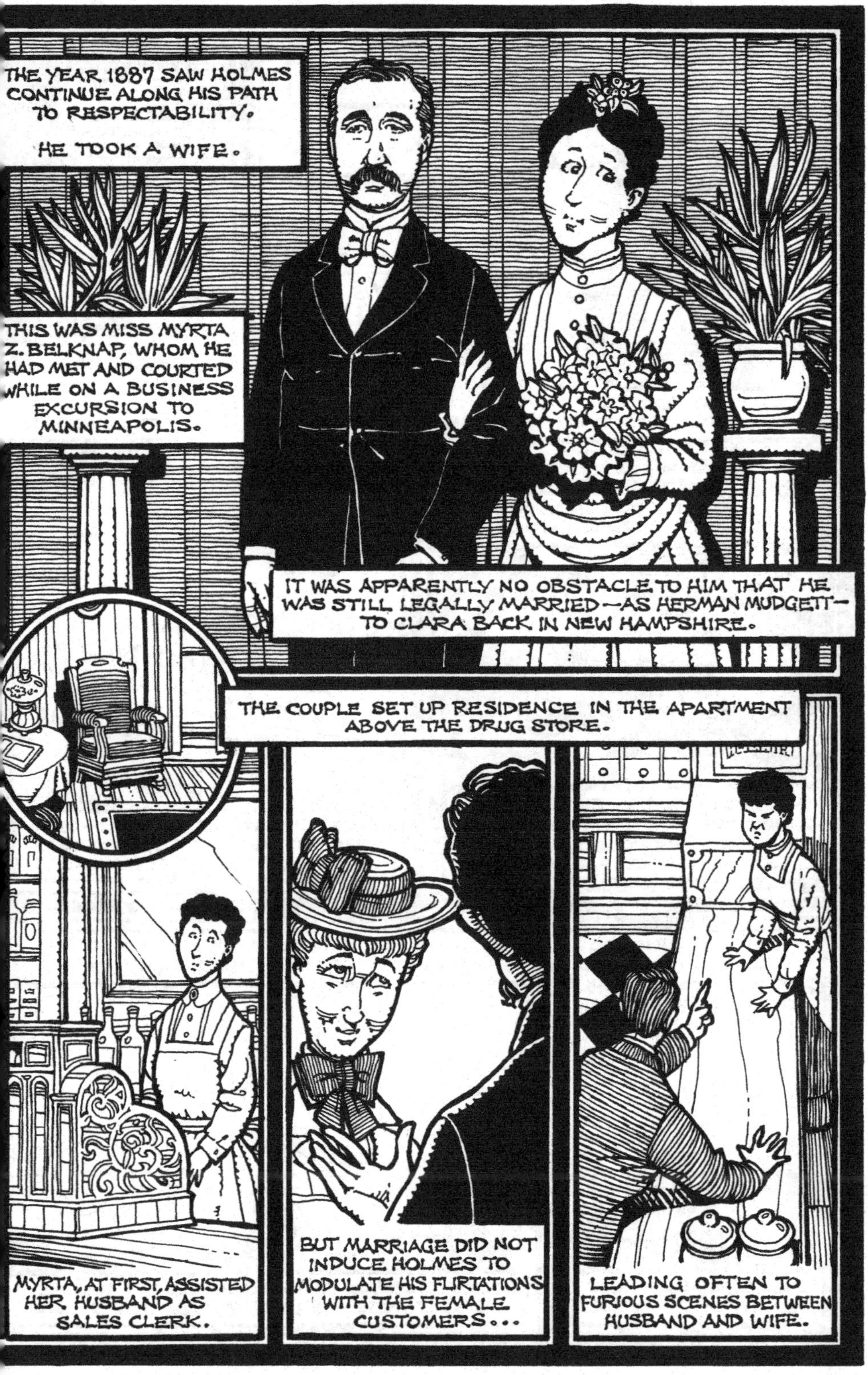
THE YEAR 1887 SAW HOLMES CONTINUE ALONG HIS PATH TO RESPECTABILITY.
HE TOOK A WIFE.
THIS WAS MISS MYRTA Z. BELKNAP, WHOM HE HAD MET AND COURTED WHILE ON A BUSINESS EXCURSION TO MINNEAPOLIS.
IT WAS APPARENTLY NO OBSTACLE TO HIM THAT HE WAS STILL LEGALLY MARRIED—AS HERMAN MUDGETT—TO CLARA BACK IN NEW HAMPSHIRE.
THE COUPLE SET UP RESIDENCE IN THE APARTMENT ABOVE THE DRUG STORE.
MYRTA, AT FIRST, ASSISTED HER HUSBAND AS SALES CLERK.
BUT MARRIAGE DID NOT INDUCE HOLMES TO MODULATE HIS FLIRTATIONS WITH THE FEMALE CUSTOMERS...
LEADING OFTEN TO FURIOUS SCENES BETWEEN HUSBAND AND WIFE.

THE PROBLEM WAS SOLVED IN THE SPRING OF 1888, WHEN MYRTA BECAME PREGNANT.

HER HUSBAND SENT HER TO LIVE WITH HER PARENTS, WHO HAD RECENTLY MOVED TO THE NORTHERN SUBURB OF WILMETTE.

THERE SHE REMAINED, EVENTUALLY GIVING BIRTH TO A DAUGHTER...

WHILE HOLMES CONTINUED HIS EXPLOITS IN ENGLEWOOD.

IN ADDITION TO THE STORE, HE RAN A THRIVING MAIL-ORDER BUSINESS IN PATENT MEDICINES, INCLUDING CURES FOR BALDNESS AND ALCOHOLISM.

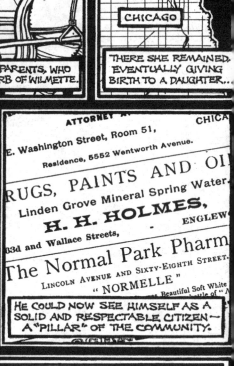

ATTORNEY A... CHICA
E. Washington Street, Room 51,
Residence, 5552 Wentworth Avenue.
RUGS, PAINTS AND OI!
Linden Grove Mineral Spring Water.
H. H. HOLMES, — ENGLEW
03d and Wallace Streets,
The Normal Park Pharm
LINCOLN AVENUE AND SIXTY-EIGHTH STREET.
" NORMELLE "
Beautiful Soft White
tle of "N

HE COULD NOW SEE HIMSELF AS A SOLID AND RESPECTABLE CITIZEN — A "PILLAR" OF THE COMMUNITY.

THE CITY OF CHICAGO WAS IN THE RUNNING TO HOST THE UPCOMING WORLD'S COLUMBIAN EXPOSITION.

ENGLEWOOD WAS NOW THE "CITY OF THE FUTURE."

THIS WAS THE TIME TO PURCHASE THE VACANT PROPERTY OPPOSITE THE DRUG STORE.

HOLMES DREAMED OF A MAGNIFICENT STRUCTURE TO BE BUILT THERE — A LANDMARK ADMIRED BY ALL.

PART II.
THE CASTLE

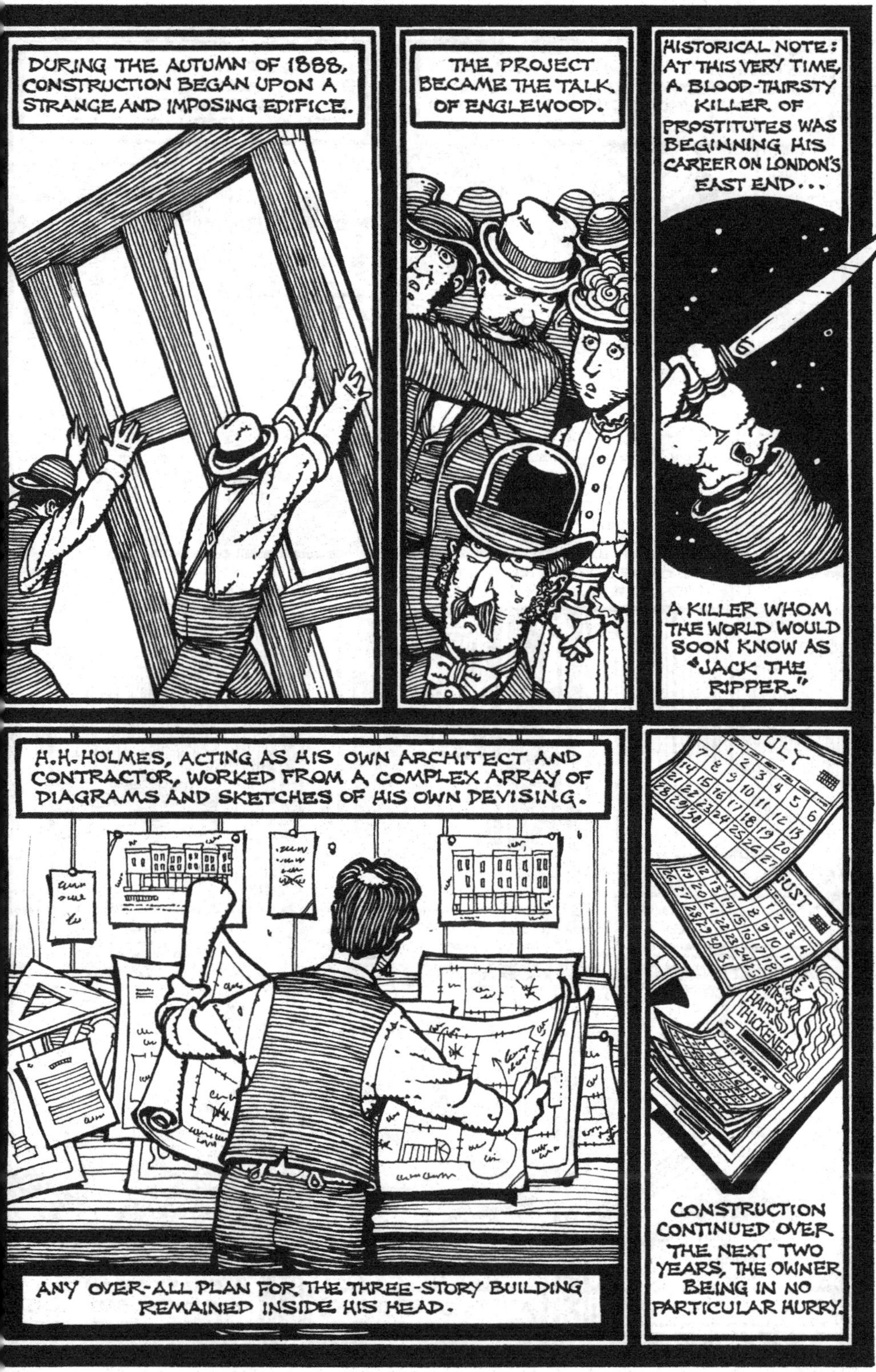
DURING THE AUTUMN OF 1888, CONSTRUCTION BEGAN UPON A STRANGE AND IMPOSING EDIFICE.
THE PROJECT BECAME THE TALK OF ENGLEWOOD.
HISTORICAL NOTE: AT THIS VERY TIME, A BLOOD-THIRSTY KILLER OF PROSTITUTES WAS BEGINNING HIS CAREER ON LONDON'S EAST END...
A KILLER WHOM THE WORLD WOULD SOON KNOW AS "JACK THE RIPPER."
H.H. HOLMES, ACTING AS HIS OWN ARCHITECT AND CONTRACTOR, WORKED FROM A COMPLEX ARRAY OF DIAGRAMS AND SKETCHES OF HIS OWN DEVISING.
ANY OVER-ALL PLAN FOR THE THREE-STORY BUILDING REMAINED INSIDE HIS HEAD.
JULY
THICKENER
CONSTRUCTION CONTINUED OVER THE NEXT TWO YEARS, THE OWNER BEING IN NO PARTICULAR HURRY.

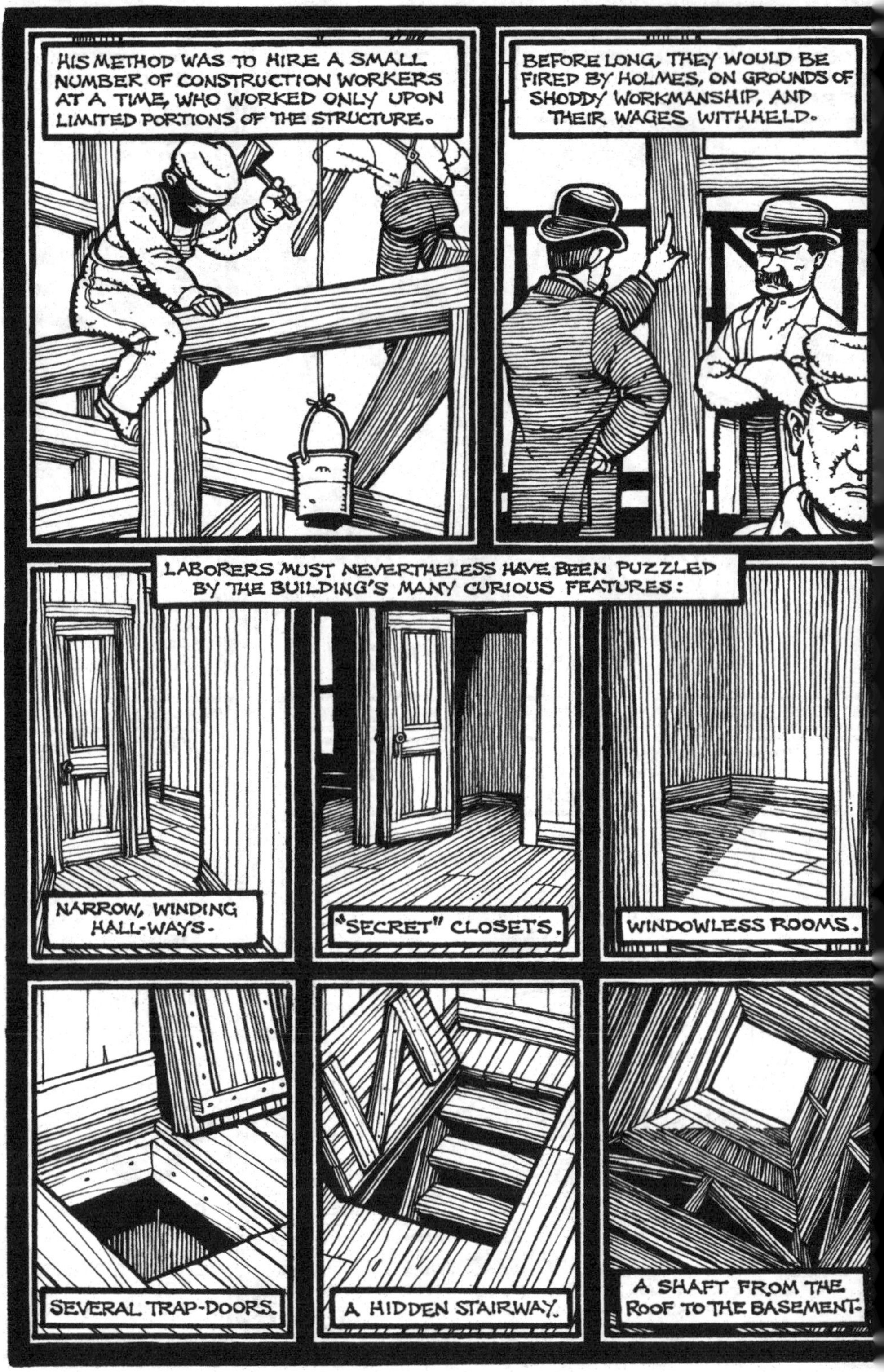
HIS METHOD WAS TO HIRE A SMALL NUMBER OF CONSTRUCTION WORKERS AT A TIME, WHO WORKED ONLY UPON LIMITED PORTIONS OF THE STRUCTURE.
BEFORE LONG, THEY WOULD BE FIRED BY HOLMES, ON GROUNDS OF SHODDY WORKMANSHIP, AND THEIR WAGES WITHHELD.
LABORERS MUST NEVERTHELESS HAVE BEEN PUZZLED BY THE BUILDING'S MANY CURIOUS FEATURES:
NARROW, WINDING HALL-WAYS.
"SECRET" CLOSETS.
WINDOWLESS ROOMS.
SEVERAL TRAP-DOORS.
A HIDDEN STAIRWAY.
A SHAFT FROM THE ROOF TO THE BASEMENT.

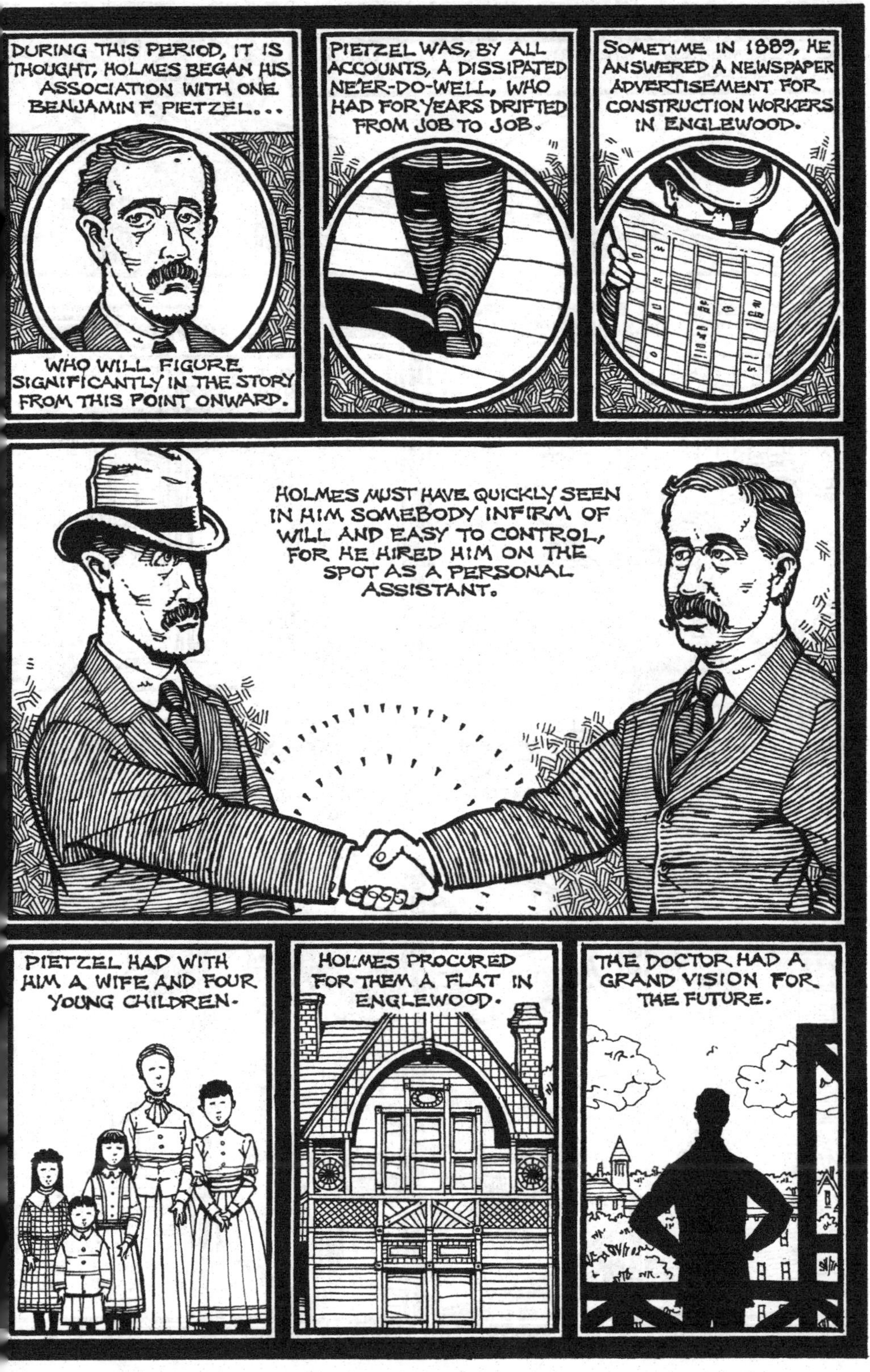
DURING THIS PERIOD, IT IS THOUGHT, HOLMES BEGAN HIS ASSOCIATION WITH ONE BENJAMIN F. PIETZEL...
WHO WILL FIGURE SIGNIFICANTLY IN THE STORY FROM THIS POINT ONWARD.
PIETZEL WAS, BY ALL ACCOUNTS, A DISSIPATED NE'ER-DO-WELL, WHO HAD FOR YEARS DRIFTED FROM JOB TO JOB.
SOMETIME IN 1889, HE ANSWERED A NEWSPAPER ADVERTISEMENT FOR CONSTRUCTION WORKERS IN ENGLEWOOD.
HOLMES MUST HAVE QUICKLY SEEN IN HIM SOMEBODY INFIRM OF WILL AND EASY TO CONTROL, FOR HE HIRED HIM ON THE SPOT AS A PERSONAL ASSISTANT.
PIETZEL HAD WITH HIM A WIFE AND FOUR YOUNG CHILDREN.
HOLMES PROCURED FOR THEM A FLAT IN ENGLEWOOD.
THE DOCTOR HAD A GRAND VISION FOR THE FUTURE.

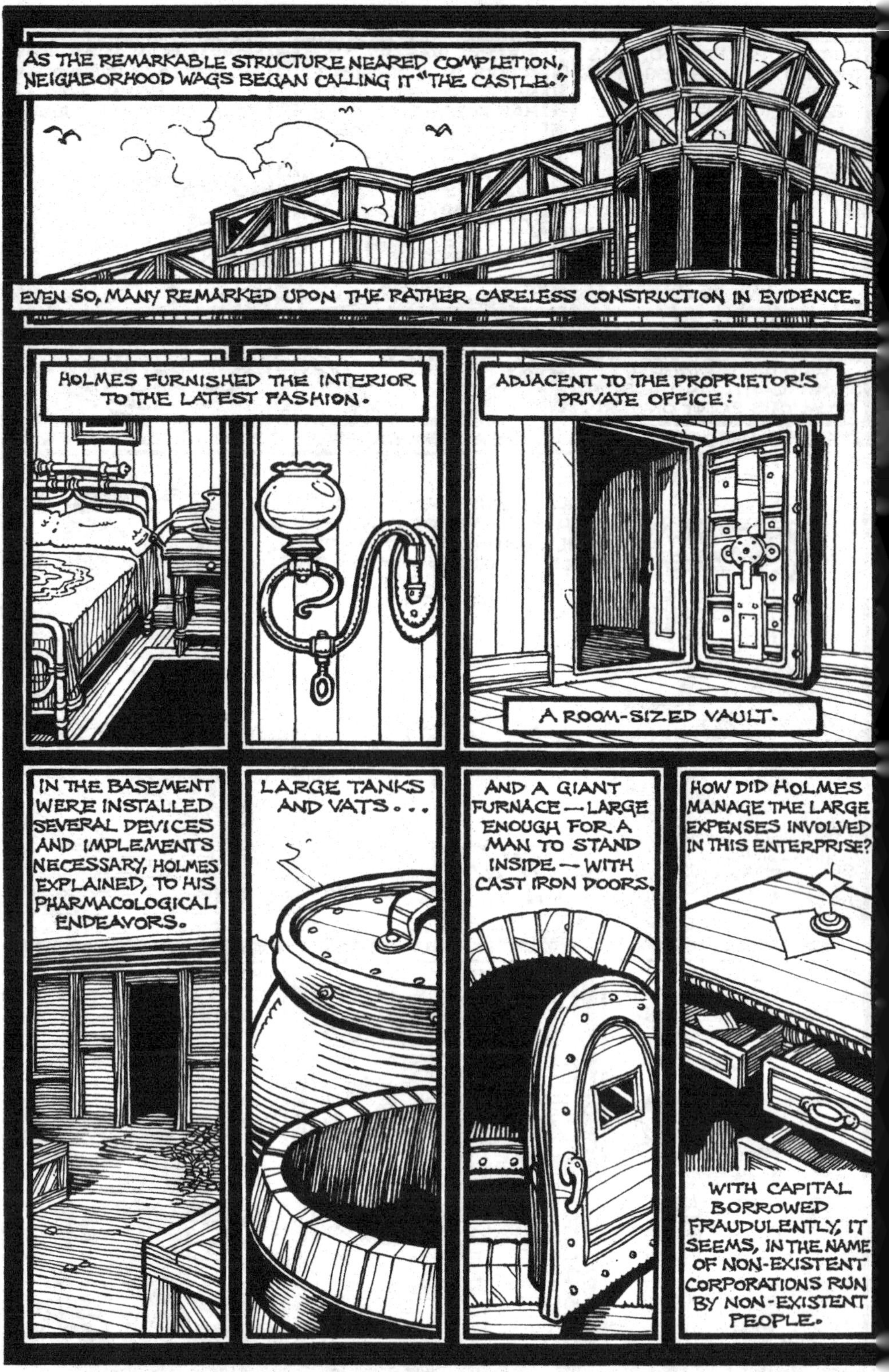
AS THE REMARKABLE STRUCTURE NEARED COMPLETION, NEIGHBORHOOD WAGS BEGAN CALLING IT "THE CASTLE."
EVEN SO, MANY REMARKED UPON THE RATHER CARELESS CONSTRUCTION IN EVIDENCE.
HOLMES FURNISHED THE INTERIOR TO THE LATEST FASHION.
ADJACENT TO THE PROPRIETOR'S PRIVATE OFFICE:
A ROOM-SIZED VAULT.
IN THE BASEMENT WERE INSTALLED SEVERAL DEVICES AND IMPLEMENTS NECESSARY, HOLMES EXPLAINED, TO HIS PHARMACOLOGICAL ENDEAVORS.
LARGE TANKS AND VATS...
AND A GIANT FURNACE — LARGE ENOUGH FOR A MAN TO STAND INSIDE — WITH CAST IRON DOORS.
HOW DID HOLMES MANAGE THE LARGE EXPENSES INVOLVED IN THIS ENTERPRISE?
WITH CAPITAL BORROWED FRAUDULENTLY, IT SEEMS, IN THE NAME OF NON-EXISTENT CORPORATIONS RUN BY NON-EXISTENT PEOPLE.

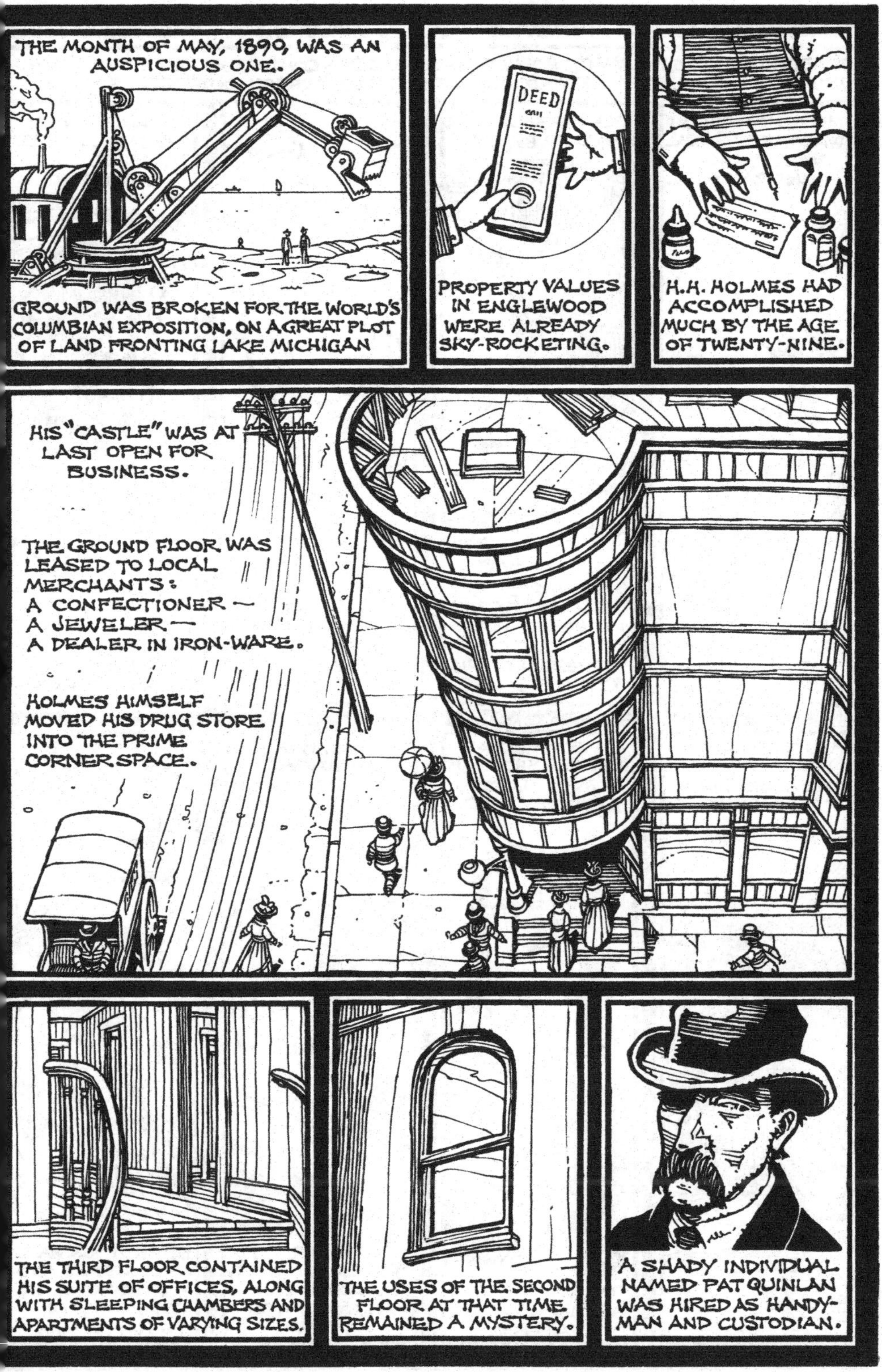
THE MONTH OF MAY, 1890, WAS AN AUSPICIOUS ONE.
GROUND WAS BROKEN FOR THE WORLD'S COLUMBIAN EXPOSITION, ON A GREAT PLOT OF LAND FRONTING LAKE MICHIGAN
DEED
PROPERTY VALUES IN ENGLEWOOD WERE ALREADY SKY-ROCKETING.
H.H. HOLMES HAD ACCOMPLISHED MUCH BY THE AGE OF TWENTY-NINE.
HIS "CASTLE" WAS AT LAST OPEN FOR BUSINESS.
...
THE GROUND FLOOR WAS LEASED TO LOCAL MERCHANTS: A CONFECTIONER — A JEWELER — A DEALER IN IRON-WARE.
...
HOLMES HIMSELF MOVED HIS DRUG STORE INTO THE PRIME CORNER SPACE.
THE THIRD FLOOR CONTAINED HIS SUITE OF OFFICES, ALONG WITH SLEEPING CHAMBERS AND APARTMENTS OF VARYING SIZES.
THE USES OF THE SECOND FLOOR AT THAT TIME REMAINED A MYSTERY.
A SHADY INDIVIDUAL NAMED PAT QUINLAN WAS HIRED AS HANDY-MAN AND CUSTODIAN.

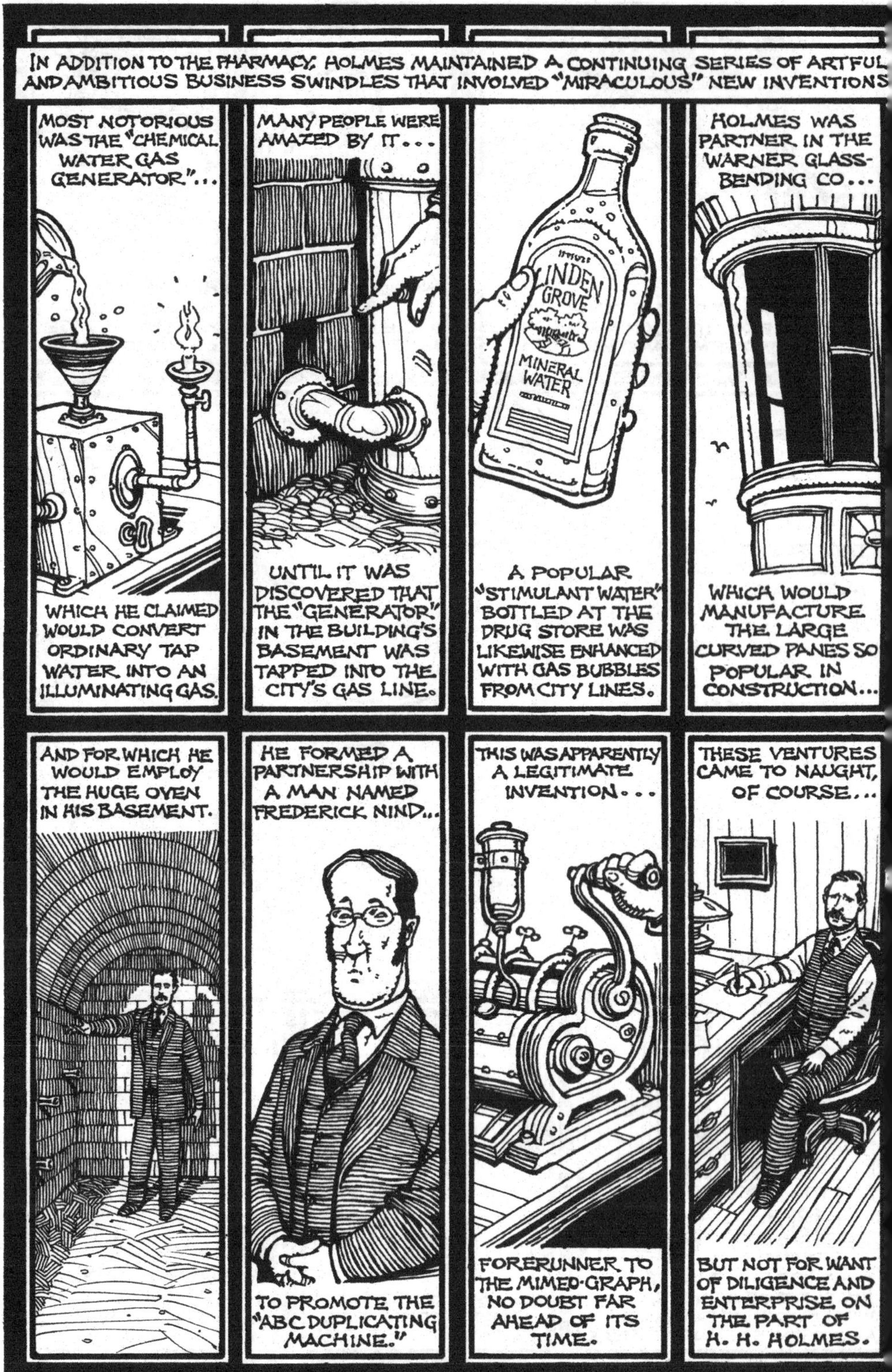
IN ADDITION TO THE PHARMACY, HOLMES MAINTAINED A CONTINUING SERIES OF ARTFUL AND AMBITIOUS BUSINESS SWINDLES THAT INVOLVED "MIRACULOUS" NEW INVENTIONS
MOST NOTORIOUS WAS THE "CHEMICAL WATER GAS GENERATOR"...
WHICH HE CLAIMED WOULD CONVERT ORDINARY TAP WATER INTO AN ILLUMINATING GAS.
MANY PEOPLE WERE AMAZED BY IT...
UNTIL IT WAS DISCOVERED THAT THE "GENERATOR" IN THE BUILDING'S BASEMENT WAS TAPPED INTO THE CITY'S GAS LINE.
LINDEN GROVE
MINERAL WATER
A POPULAR "STIMULANT WATER" BOTTLED AT THE DRUG STORE WAS LIKEWISE ENHANCED WITH GAS BUBBLES FROM CITY LINES.
HOLMES WAS PARTNER IN THE WARNER GLASS-BENDING CO...
WHICH WOULD MANUFACTURE THE LARGE CURVED PANES SO POPULAR IN CONSTRUCTION...
AND FOR WHICH HE WOULD EMPLOY THE HUGE OVEN IN HIS BASEMENT.
HE FORMED A PARTNERSHIP WITH A MAN NAMED FREDERICK NIND...
TO PROMOTE THE "ABC DUPLICATING MACHINE."
THIS WAS APPARENTLY A LEGITIMATE INVENTION...
FORERUNNER TO THE MIMEO-GRAPH, NO DOUBT FAR AHEAD OF ITS TIME.
THESE VENTURES CAME TO NAUGHT, OF COURSE...
BUT NOT FOR WANT OF DILIGENCE AND ENTERPRISE ON THE PART OF H. H. HOLMES.

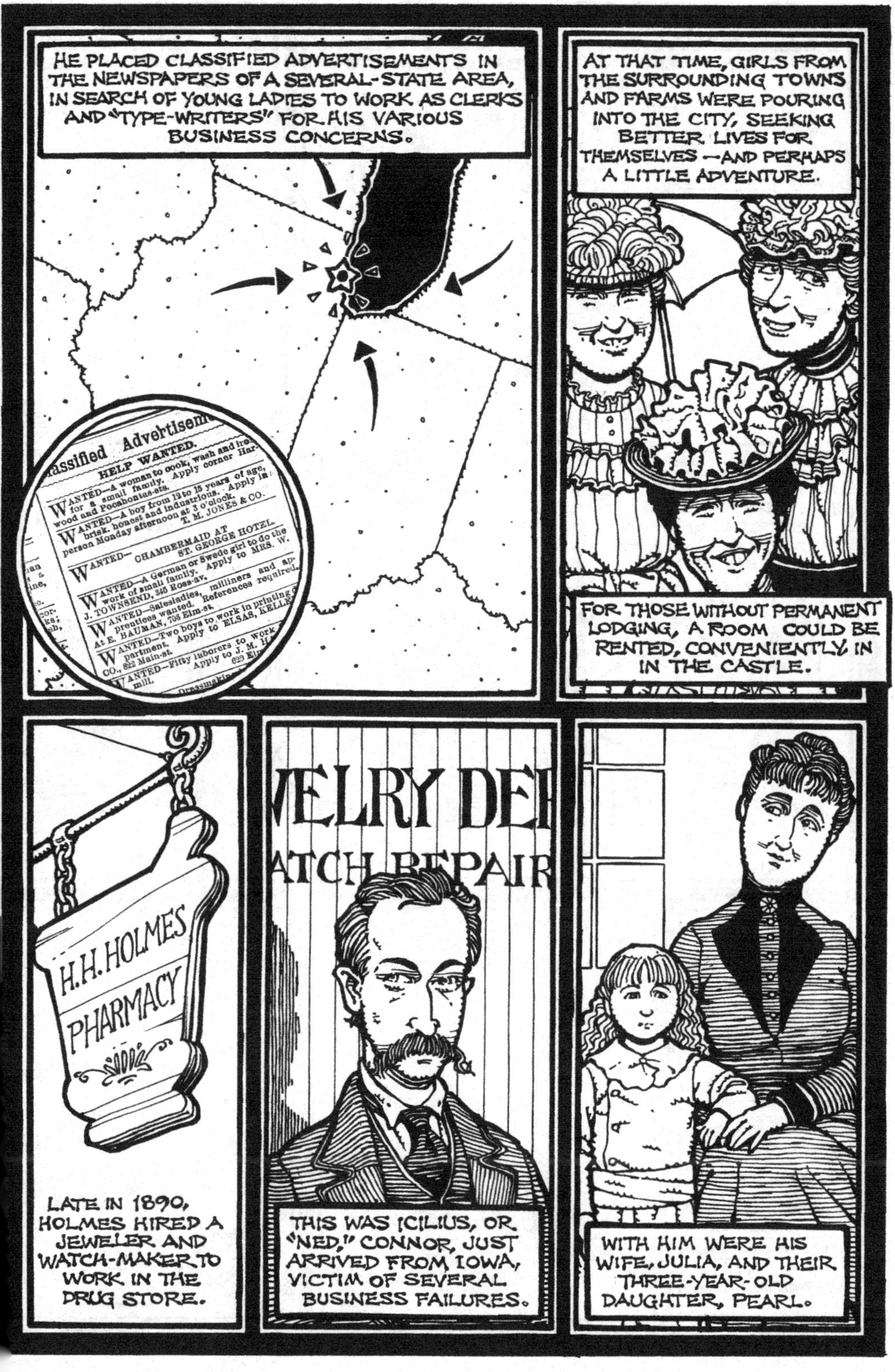
HE PLACED CLASSIFIED ADVERTISEMENTS IN THE NEWSPAPERS OF A SEVERAL-STATE AREA, IN SEARCH OF YOUNG LADIES TO WORK AS CLERKS AND "TYPE-WRITERS" FOR HIS VARIOUS BUSINESS CONCERNS.
lassified Advertisem
HELP WANTED.
AT THAT TIME, GIRLS FROM THE SURROUNDING TOWNS AND FARMS WERE POURING INTO THE CITY, SEEKING BETTER LIVES FOR THEMSELVES —AND PERHAPS A LITTLE ADVENTURE.
FOR THOSE WITHOUT PERMANENT LODGING, A ROOM COULD BE RENTED, CONVENIENTLY, IN IN THE CASTLE.
H.H. HOLMES
PHARMACY
LATE IN 1890, HOLMES HIRED A JEWELER AND WATCH-MAKER TO WORK IN THE DRUG STORE.
VELRY DE
ATCH REPAIR
THIS WAS ICILIUS, OR "NED," CONNOR, JUST ARRIVED FROM IOWA, VICTIM OF SEVERAL BUSINESS FAILURES.
WITH HIM WERE HIS WIFE, JULIA, AND THEIR THREE-YEAR-OLD DAUGHTER, PEARL.

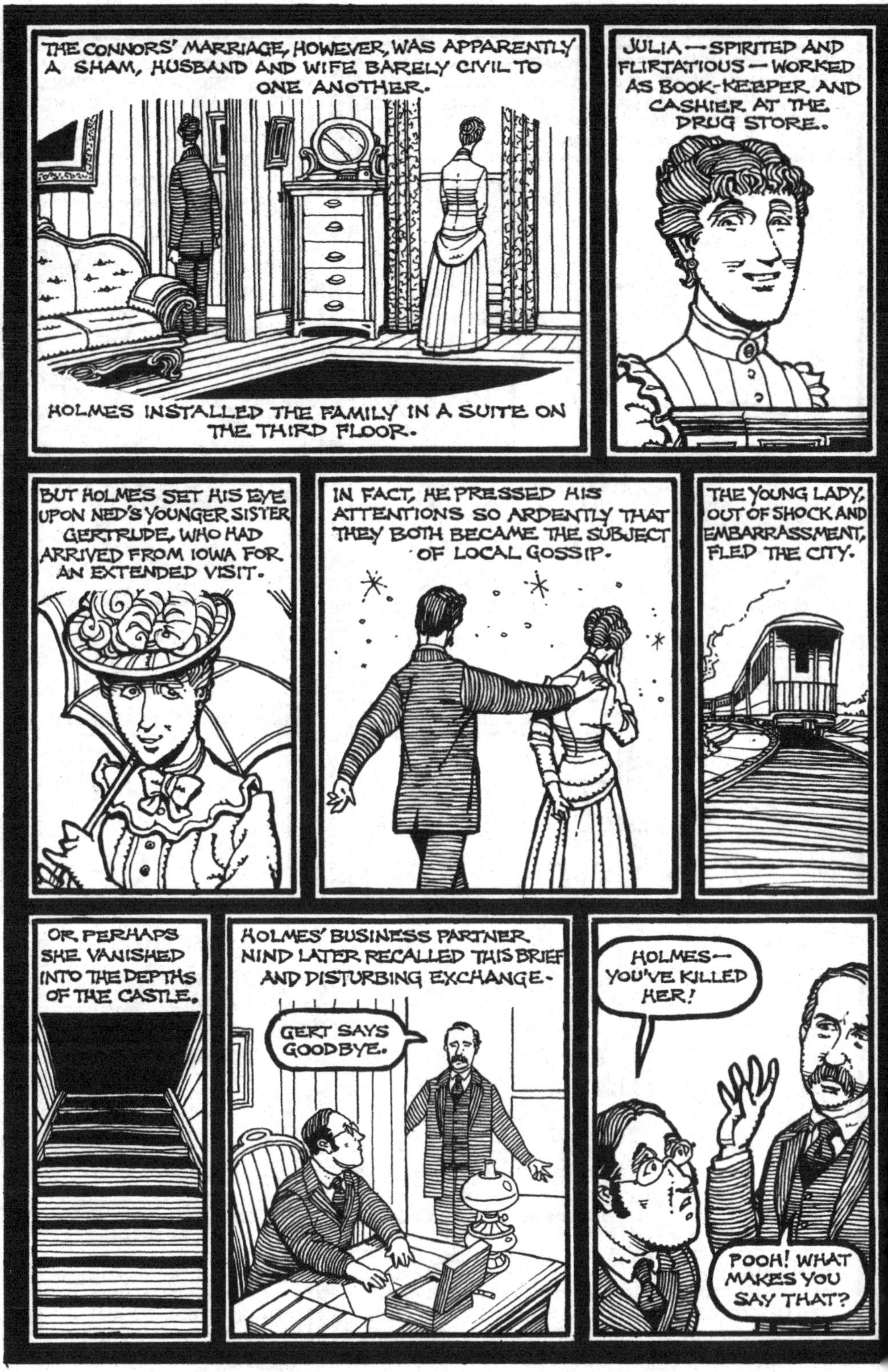
THE CONNORS' MARRIAGE, HOWEVER, WAS APPARENTLY A SHAM, HUSBAND AND WIFE BARELY CIVIL TO ONE ANOTHER.
HOLMES INSTALLED THE FAMILY IN A SUITE ON THE THIRD FLOOR.
JULIA — SPIRITED AND FLIRTATIOUS — WORKED AS BOOK-KEEPER AND CASHIER AT THE DRUG STORE.
BUT HOLMES SET HIS EYE UPON NED'S YOUNGER SISTER GERTRUDE, WHO HAD ARRIVED FROM IOWA FOR AN EXTENDED VISIT.
IN FACT, HE PRESSED HIS ATTENTIONS SO ARDENTLY THAT THEY BOTH BECAME THE SUBJECT OF LOCAL GOSSIP.
THE YOUNG LADY, OUT OF SHOCK AND EMBARRASSMENT, FLED THE CITY.
OR PERHAPS SHE VANISHED INTO THE DEPTHS OF THE CASTLE.
HOLMES' BUSINESS PARTNER NIND LATER RECALLED THIS BRIEF AND DISTURBING EXCHANGE.
GERT SAYS GOODBYE.
HOLMES— YOU'VE KILLED HER!
POOH! WHAT MAKES YOU SAY THAT?

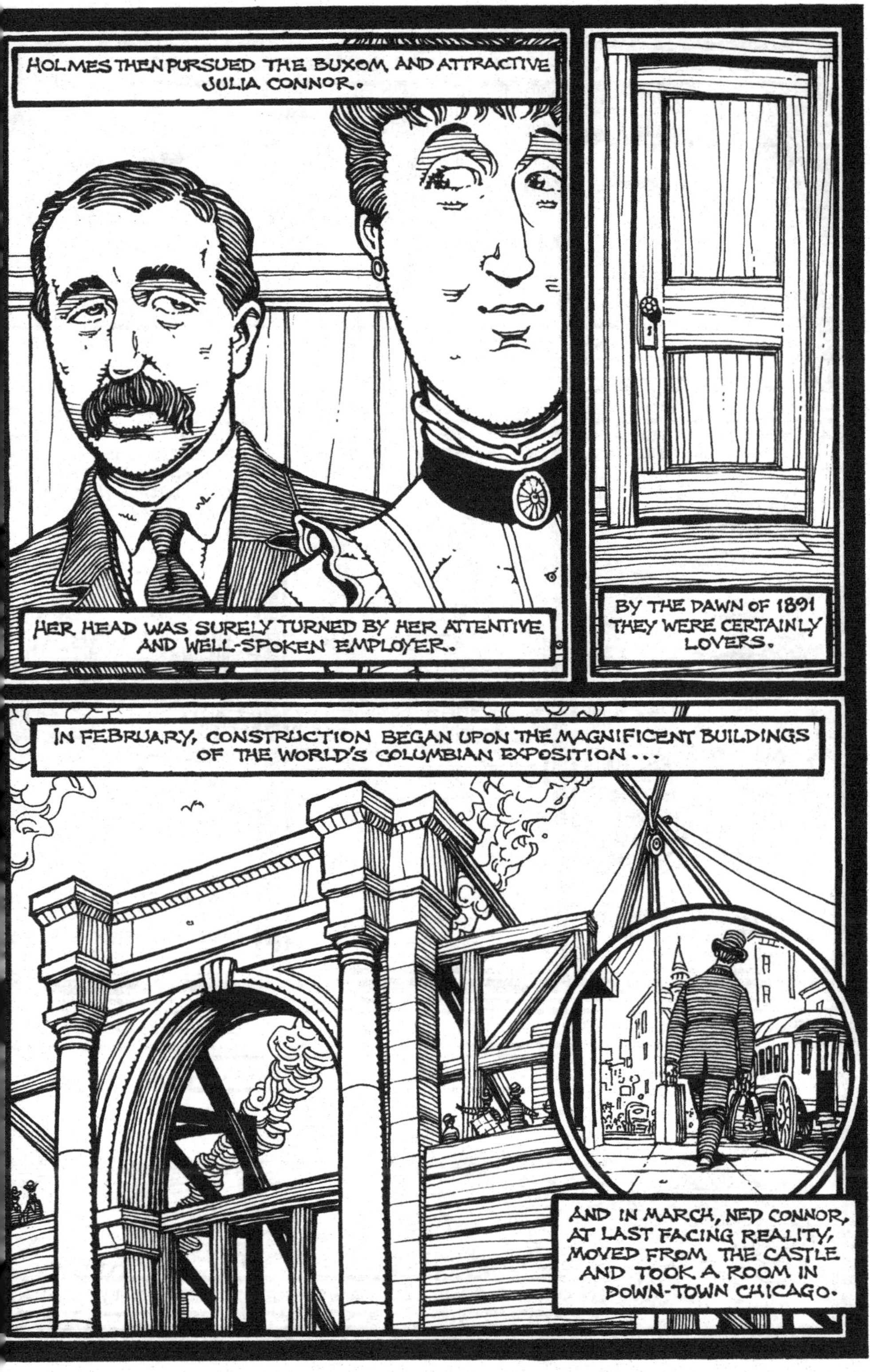
HOLMES THEN PURSUED THE BUXOM AND ATTRACTIVE JULIA CONNOR.
HER HEAD WAS SURELY TURNED BY HER ATTENTIVE AND WELL-SPOKEN EMPLOYER.
BY THE DAWN OF 1891 THEY WERE CERTAINLY LOVERS.
IN FEBRUARY, CONSTRUCTION BEGAN UPON THE MAGNIFICENT BUILDINGS OF THE WORLD'S COLUMBIAN EXPOSITION...
AND IN MARCH, NED CONNOR, AT LAST FACING REALITY, MOVED FROM THE CASTLE AND TOOK A ROOM IN DOWN-TOWN CHICAGO.

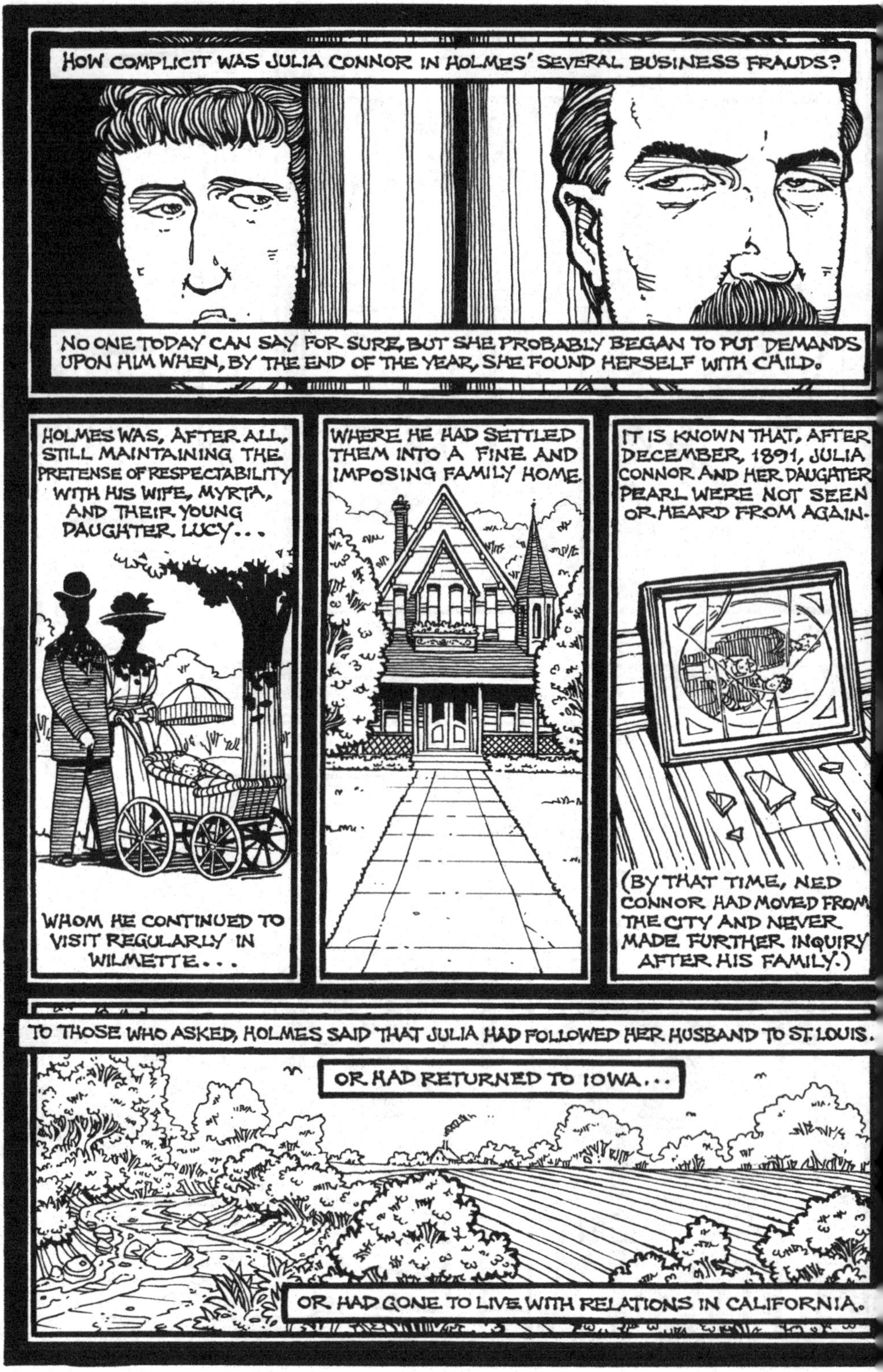
HOW COMPLICIT WAS JULIA CONNOR IN HOLMES' SEVERAL BUSINESS FRAUDS?
NO ONE TODAY CAN SAY FOR SURE, BUT SHE PROBABLY BEGAN TO PUT DEMANDS UPON HIM WHEN, BY THE END OF THE YEAR, SHE FOUND HERSELF WITH CHILD.
HOLMES WAS, AFTER ALL, STILL MAINTAINING THE PRETENSE OF RESPECTABILITY WITH HIS WIFE, MYRTA, AND THEIR YOUNG DAUGHTER LUCY...
WHOM HE CONTINUED TO VISIT REGULARLY IN WILMETTE...
WHERE HE HAD SETTLED THEM INTO A FINE AND IMPOSING FAMILY HOME.
IT IS KNOWN THAT, AFTER DECEMBER, 1891, JULIA CONNOR AND HER DAUGHTER PEARL WERE NOT SEEN OR HEARD FROM AGAIN.
(BY THAT TIME, NED CONNOR HAD MOVED FROM THE CITY AND NEVER MADE FURTHER INQUIRY AFTER HIS FAMILY.)
TO THOSE WHO ASKED, HOLMES SAID THAT JULIA HAD FOLLOWED HER HUSBAND TO ST. LOUIS.
OR HAD RETURNED TO IOWA...
OR HAD GONE TO LIVE WITH RELATIONS IN CALIFORNIA.

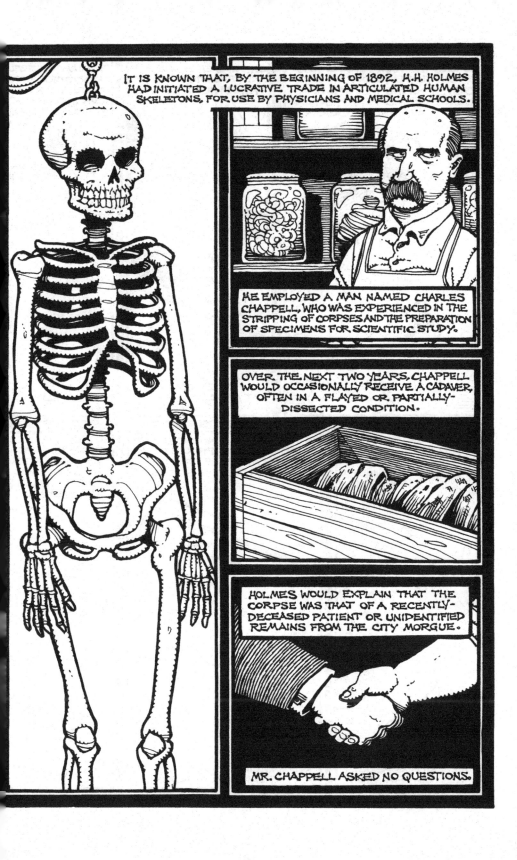

IT IS KNOWN THAT, BY THE BEGINNING OF 1892, H.H. HOLMES HAD INITIATED A LUCRATIVE TRADE IN ARTICULATED HUMAN SKELETONS, FOR USE BY PHYSICIANS AND MEDICAL SCHOOLS.

HE EMPLOYED A MAN NAMED CHARLES CHAPPELL, WHO WAS EXPERIENCED IN THE STRIPPING OF CORPSES AND THE PREPARATION OF SPECIMENS FOR SCIENTIFIC STUDY.

OVER THE NEXT TWO YEARS, CHAPPELL WOULD OCCASIONALLY RECEIVE A CADAVER, OFTEN IN A FLAYED OR PARTIALLY-DISSECTED CONDITION.

HOLMES WOULD EXPLAIN THAT THE CORPSE WAS THAT OF A RECENTLY-DECEASED PATIENT OR UNIDENTIFIED REMAINS FROM THE CITY MORGUE.

MR. CHAPPELL ASKED NO QUESTIONS.

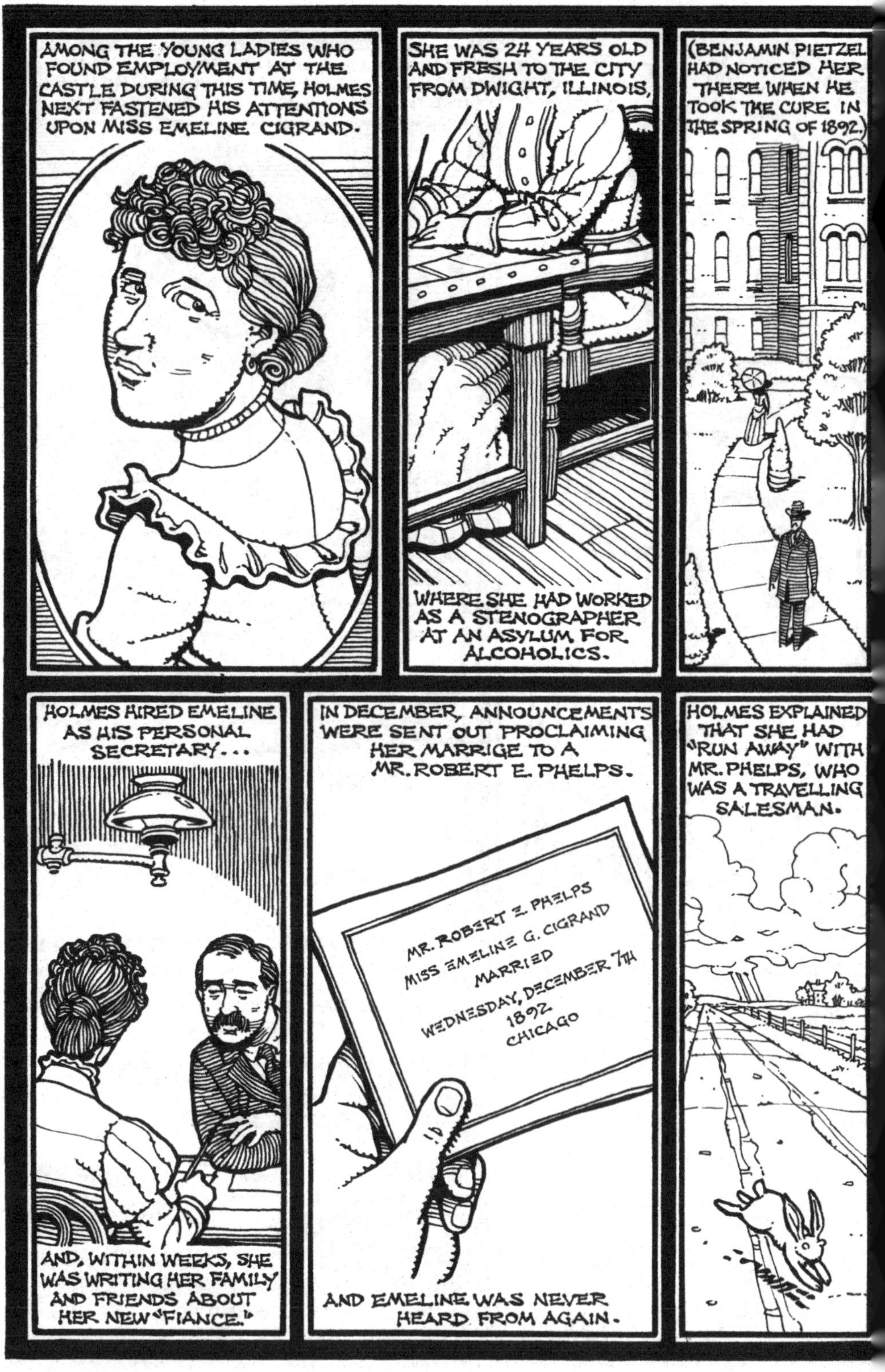
AMONG THE YOUNG LADIES WHO FOUND EMPLOYMENT AT THE CASTLE DURING THIS TIME, HOLMES NEXT FASTENED HIS ATTENTIONS UPON MISS EMELINE CIGRAND.
SHE WAS 24 YEARS OLD AND FRESH TO THE CITY FROM DWIGHT, ILLINOIS,
WHERE SHE HAD WORKED AS A STENOGRAPHER AT AN ASYLUM FOR ALCOHOLICS.
(BENJAMIN PIETZEL HAD NOTICED HER THERE WHEN HE TOOK THE CURE IN THE SPRING OF 1892.)
HOLMES HIRED EMELINE AS HIS PERSONAL SECRETARY...
AND, WITHIN WEEKS, SHE WAS WRITING HER FAMILY AND FRIENDS ABOUT HER NEW "FIANCE."
IN DECEMBER, ANNOUNCEMENTS WERE SENT OUT PROCLAIMING HER MARRIGE TO A MR. ROBERT E. PHELPS.
MR. ROBERT E. PHELPS
MISS EMELINE G. CIGRAND
MARRIED
WEDNESDAY, DECEMBER 7TH
1892
CHICAGO
AND EMELINE WAS NEVER HEARD FROM AGAIN.
HOLMES EXPLAINED THAT SHE HAD "RUN AWAY" WITH MR. PHELPS, WHO WAS A TRAVELLING SALESMAN.

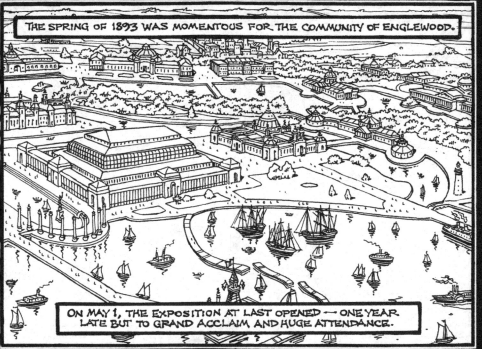

THE SPRING OF 1893 WAS MOMENTOUS FOR THE COMMUNITY OF ENGLEWOOD.

ON MAY 1, THE EXPOSITION AT LAST OPENED — ONE YEAR LATE BUT TO GRAND ACCLAIM AND HUGE ATTENDANCE.

GREAT CROWDS SWARMED INTO THE CHICAGO AREA.

TRAINS AND FERRIES BROUGHT THOUSANDS DAILY TO THE EXPOSITION GROUNDS.

THE "FERRIS" WHEEL WAS A MAJOR ATTRACTION.

MILLIONS OF ELECTRIC BULBS TURNED NIGHT INTO DAY.

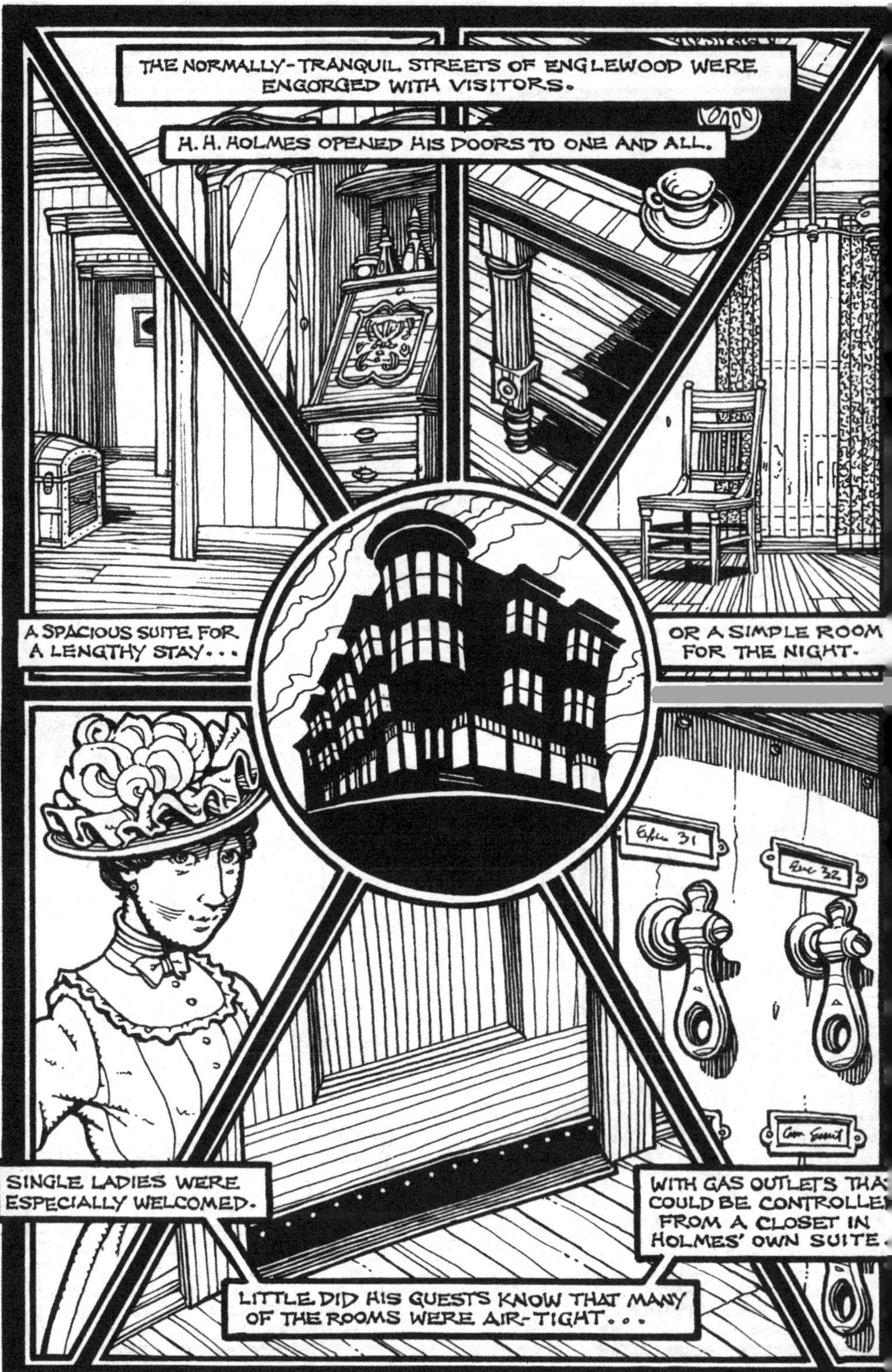
THE NORMALLY-TRANQUIL STREETS OF ENGLEWOOD WERE ENGORGED WITH VISITORS.
H. H. HOLMES OPENED HIS DOORS TO ONE AND ALL.
A SPACIOUS SUITE FOR A LENGTHY STAY...
OR A SIMPLE ROOM FOR THE NIGHT.
SINGLE LADIES WERE ESPECIALLY WELCOMED.
LITTLE DID HIS GUESTS KNOW THAT MANY OF THE ROOMS WERE AIR-TIGHT...
WITH GAS OUTLETS THA COULD BE CONTROLLE FROM A CLOSET IN HOLMES' OWN SUITE.

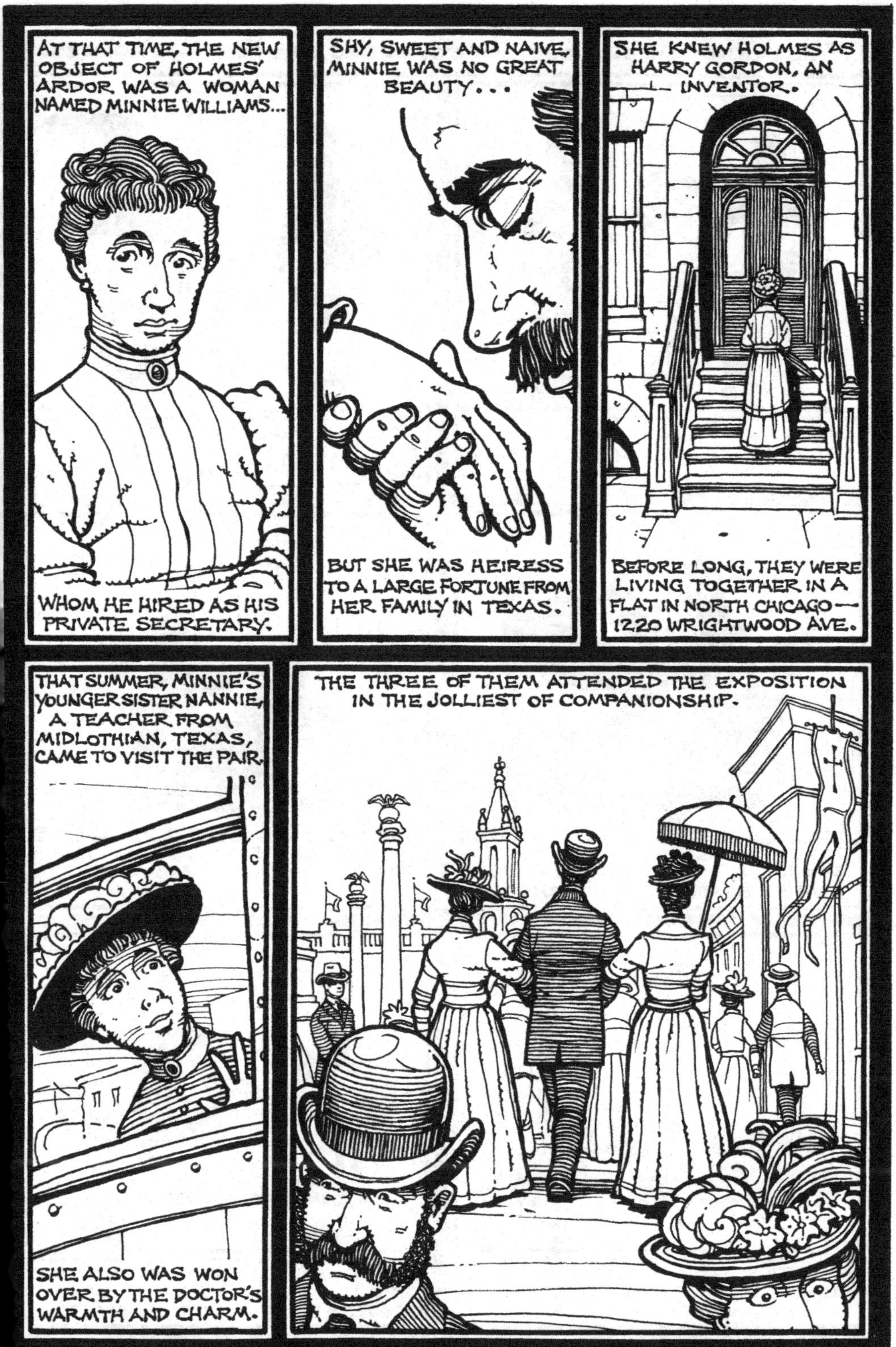
AT THAT TIME, THE NEW OBJECT OF HOLMES' ARDOR WAS A WOMAN NAMED MINNIE WILLIAMS...
WHOM HE HIRED AS HIS PRIVATE SECRETARY.
SHY, SWEET AND NAIVE, MINNIE WAS NO GREAT BEAUTY...
BUT SHE WAS HEIRESS TO A LARGE FORTUNE FROM HER FAMILY IN TEXAS.
SHE KNEW HOLMES AS HARRY GORDON, AN INVENTOR.
BEFORE LONG, THEY WERE LIVING TOGETHER IN A FLAT IN NORTH CHICAGO— 1220 WRIGHTWOOD AVE.
THAT SUMMER, MINNIE'S YOUNGER SISTER NANNIE, A TEACHER FROM MIDLOTHIAN, TEXAS, CAME TO VISIT THE PAIR.
SHE ALSO WAS WON OVER BY THE DOCTOR'S WARMTH AND CHARM.
THE THREE OF THEM ATTENDED THE EXPOSITION IN THE JOLLIEST OF COMPANIONSHIP.

THIS PERIOD WAS NO DOUBT AN EXHAUSTING ONE FOR H.H. HOLMES.

ASIDE FROM ATTENDING TO THE NEEDS OF THE WILLIAMS SISTERS...

HE CONTINUED HIS PERIODIC VISITS TO WILMETTE, FOR MAINTENANCE OF DOMESTIC BLISS WITH WIFE AND DAUGHTER.

THERE WAS THE BUSY DRUG STORE TO ADMINISTER, AS WELL AS HIS SEVERAL OTHER BUSINESS CONCERNS...

WITH ALL OF THEIR ATTENDANT CLERKS, SECRETARIES AND STENOGRAPHERS.

IN ADDITION WAS THE ROOMING HOUSE, SERVING A STREAM OF GUESTS FROM ALL OVER THE NATION.

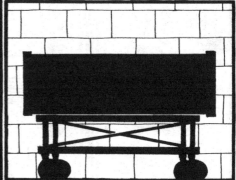

WE ARE LEFT TO WONDER HOW HE FOUND THE TIME TO CONTINUE SUPPLYING CADAVERS TO THE INDUSTRIOUS CHAPPELL.

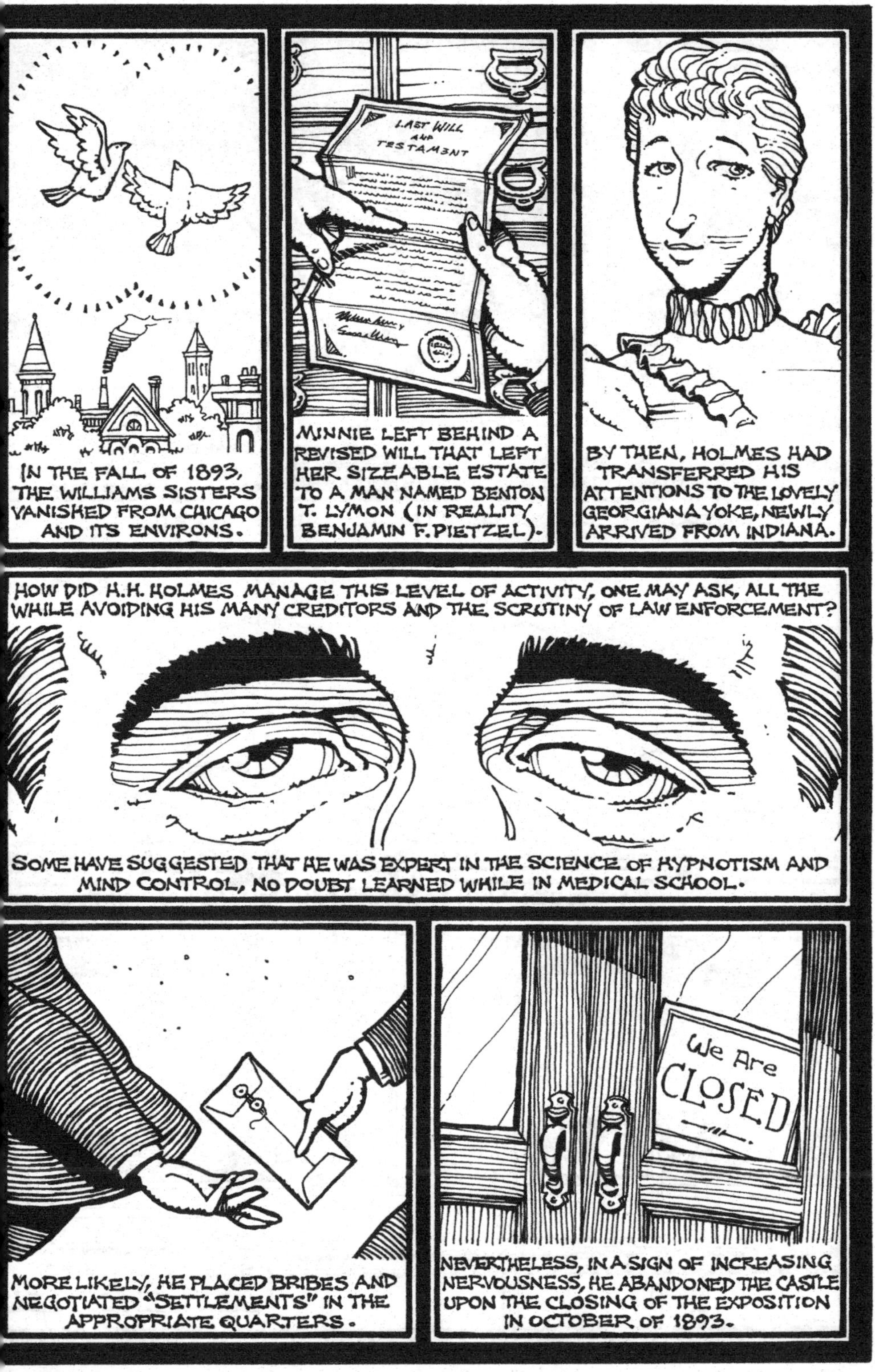
IN THE FALL OF 1893, THE WILLIAMS SISTERS VANISHED FROM CHICAGO AND ITS ENVIRONS.
LAST WILL AND TESTAMENT
MINNIE LEFT BEHIND A REVISED WILL THAT LEFT HER SIZEABLE ESTATE TO A MAN NAMED BENTON T. LYMON (IN REALITY BENJAMIN F. PIETZEL).
BY THEN, HOLMES HAD TRANSFERRED HIS ATTENTIONS TO THE LOVELY GEORGIANA YOKE, NEWLY ARRIVED FROM INDIANA.
HOW DID H.H. HOLMES MANAGE THIS LEVEL OF ACTIVITY, ONE MAY ASK, ALL THE WHILE AVOIDING HIS MANY CREDITORS AND THE SCRUTINY OF LAW ENFORCEMENT?
SOME HAVE SUGGESTED THAT HE WAS EXPERT IN THE SCIENCE OF HYPNOTISM AND MIND CONTROL, NO DOUBT LEARNED WHILE IN MEDICAL SCHOOL.
MORE LIKELY, HE PLACED BRIBES AND NEGOTIATED "SETTLEMENTS" IN THE APPROPRIATE QUARTERS.
We Are CLOSED
NEVERTHELESS, IN A SIGN OF INCREASING NERVOUSNESS, HE ABANDONED THE CASTLE UPON THE CLOSING OF THE EXPOSITION IN OCTOBER OF 1893.

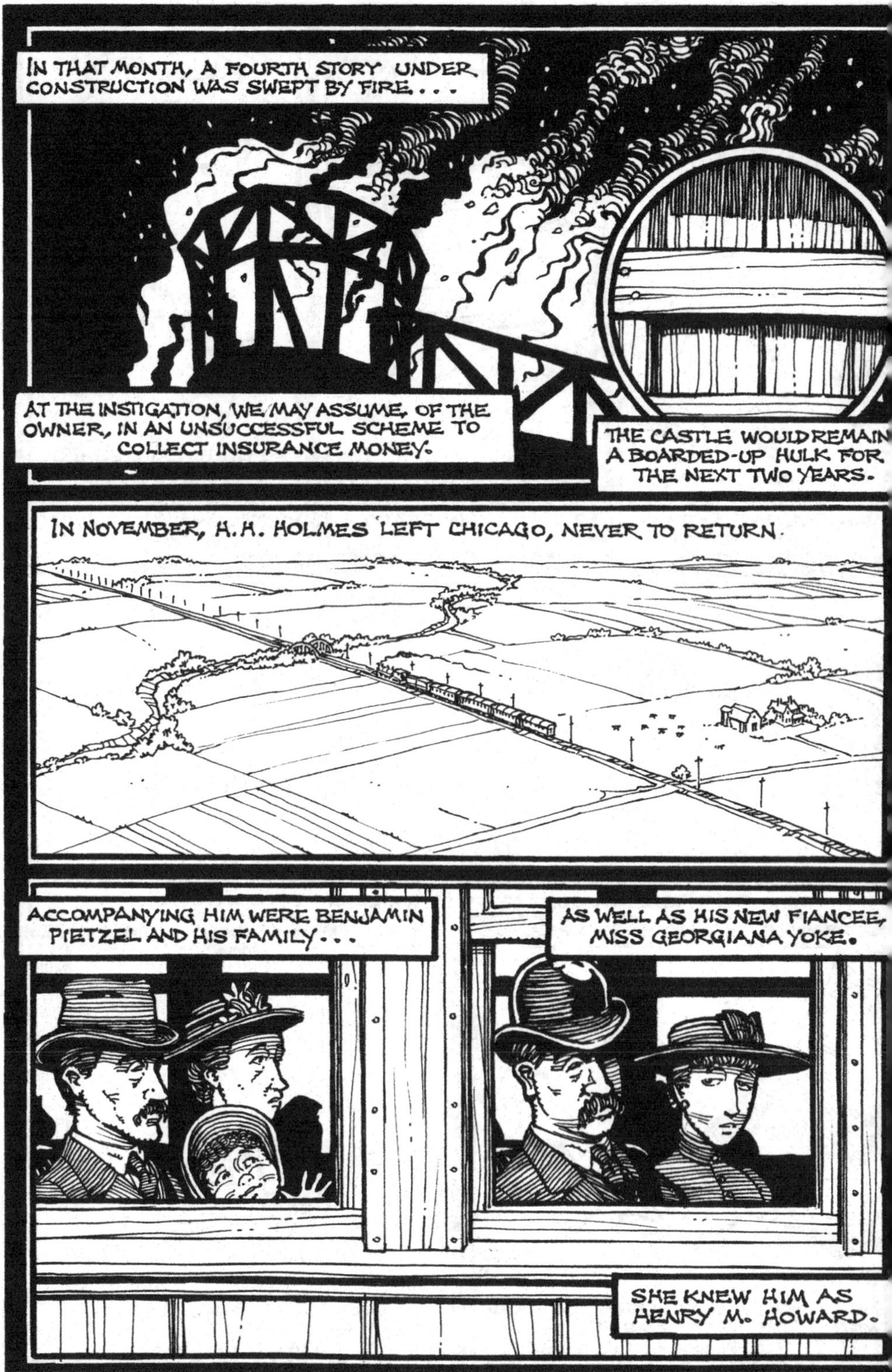
IN THAT MONTH, A FOURTH STORY UNDER CONSTRUCTION WAS SWEPT BY FIRE...
AT THE INSTIGATION, WE MAY ASSUME, OF THE OWNER, IN AN UNSUCCESSFUL SCHEME TO COLLECT INSURANCE MONEY.
THE CASTLE WOULD REMAIN A BOARDED-UP HULK FOR THE NEXT TWO YEARS.
IN NOVEMBER, H.H. HOLMES LEFT CHICAGO, NEVER TO RETURN.
ACCOMPANYING HIM WERE BENJAMIN PIETZEL AND HIS FAMILY...
AS WELL AS HIS NEW FIANCEE, MISS GEORGIANA YOKE.
SHE KNEW HIM AS HENRY M. HOWARD.

PART III.

THE DESPERATE JOURNEY

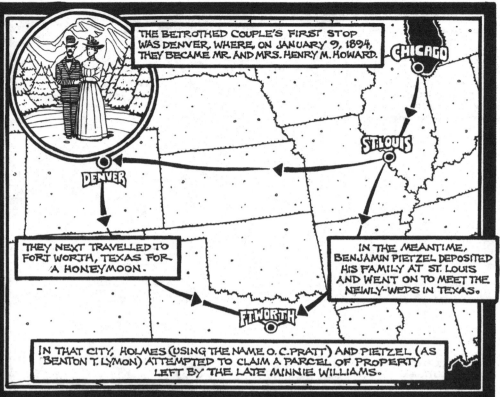

THE BETROTHED COUPLE'S FIRST STOP WAS DENVER, WHERE, ON JANUARY 9, 1894, THEY BECAME MR. AND MRS. HENRY M. HOWARD.

CHICAGO

St. LOUIS

DENVER

THEY NEXT TRAVELLED TO FORT WORTH, TEXAS FOR A HONEYMOON.

IN THE MEANTIME, BENJAMIN PIETZEL DEPOSITED HIS FAMILY AT ST. LOUIS AND WENT ON TO MEET THE NEWLY-WEDS IN TEXAS.

FT.WORTH

IN THAT CITY, HOLMES (USING THE NAME O. C. PRATT) AND PIETZEL (AS BENTON T. LYMON) ATTEMPTED TO CLAIM A PARCEL OF PROPERTY LEFT BY THE LATE MINNIE WILLIAMS.

THEY ALSO INITIATED A SCHEME TO STEAL A LARGE NUMBER OF HORSES...

BUT IMMINENT CAPTURE FORCED THEM, BY MAY, TO LEAVE TOWN.

THEY RESETTLED IN ST. LOUIS, WHERE HOLMES LOST NO TIME IN ATTEMPTING ANOTHER SWINDLE — THIS INVOLVING A SMALL DRUG STORE AND ITS INVENTORY.

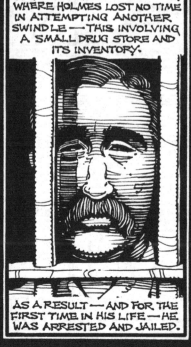

AS A RESULT — AND FOR THE FIRST TIME IN HIS LIFE — HE WAS ARRESTED AND JAILED.

TO HIS TRUSTING BRIDE, WHO BELIEVED HIM AN HONEST, HARD-WORKING BUSINESSMAN, HE SAID THAT HE WAS VICTIM TO THE LIES AND FALSE ACCUSATIONS OF JEALOUS COMPETITORS.

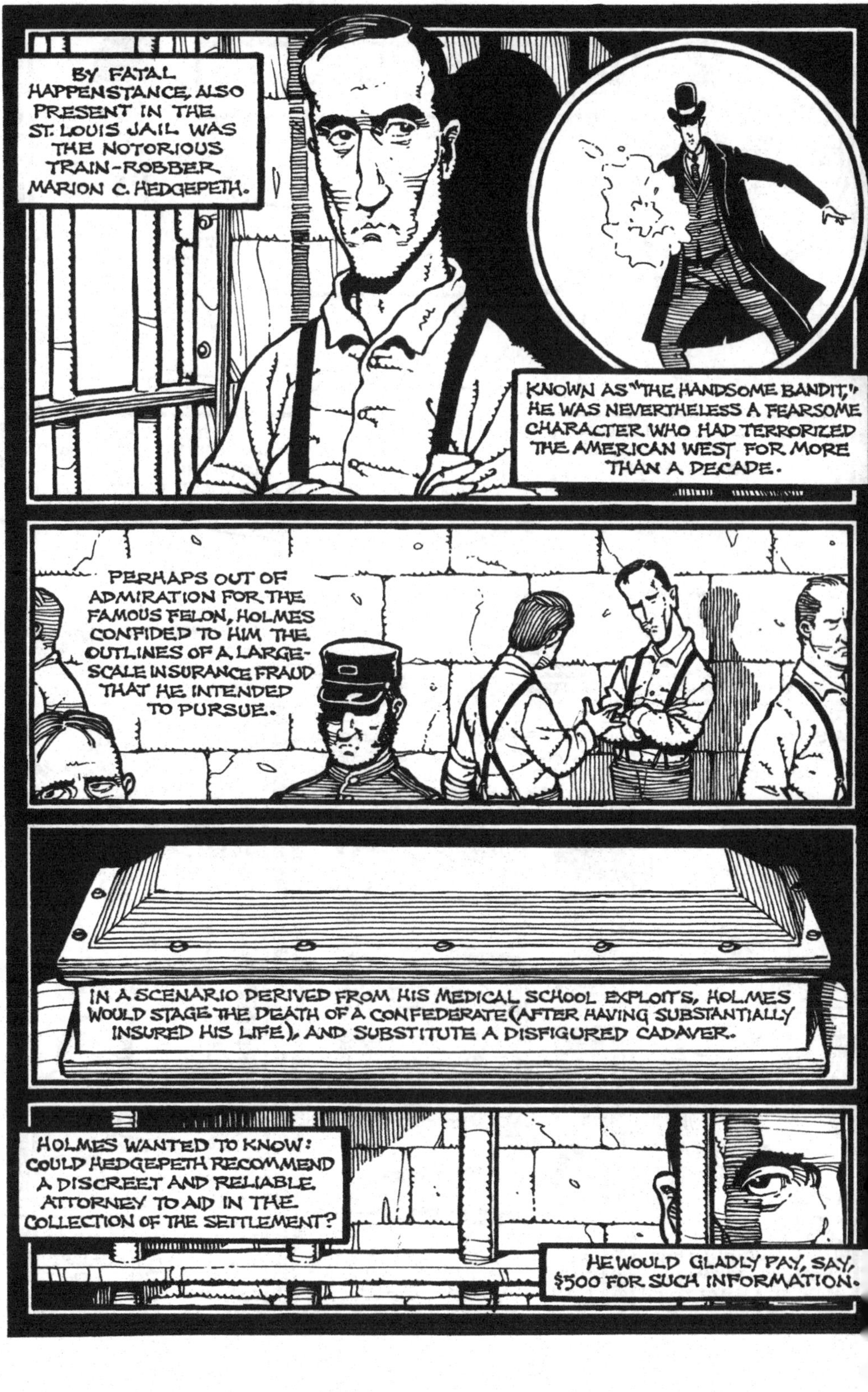
BY FATAL HAPPENSTANCE, ALSO PRESENT IN THE ST. LOUIS JAIL WAS THE NOTORIOUS TRAIN-ROBBER MARION C. HEDGEPETH.
KNOWN AS "THE HANDSOME BANDIT," HE WAS NEVERTHELESS A FEARSOME CHARACTER WHO HAD TERRORIZED THE AMERICAN WEST FOR MORE THAN A DECADE.
PERHAPS OUT OF ADMIRATION FOR THE FAMOUS FELON, HOLMES CONFIDED TO HIM THE OUTLINES OF A LARGE-SCALE INSURANCE FRAUD THAT HE INTENDED TO PURSUE.
IN A SCENARIO DERIVED FROM HIS MEDICAL SCHOOL EXPLOITS, HOLMES WOULD STAGE THE DEATH OF A CONFEDERATE (AFTER HAVING SUBSTANTIALLY INSURED HIS LIFE), AND SUBSTITUTE A DISFIGURED CADAVER.
HOLMES WANTED TO KNOW: COULD HEDGEPETH RECOMMEND A DISCREET AND RELIABLE ATTORNEY TO AID IN THE COLLECTION OF THE SETTLEMENT?
HE WOULD GLADLY PAY, SAY, $500 FOR SUCH INFORMATION.

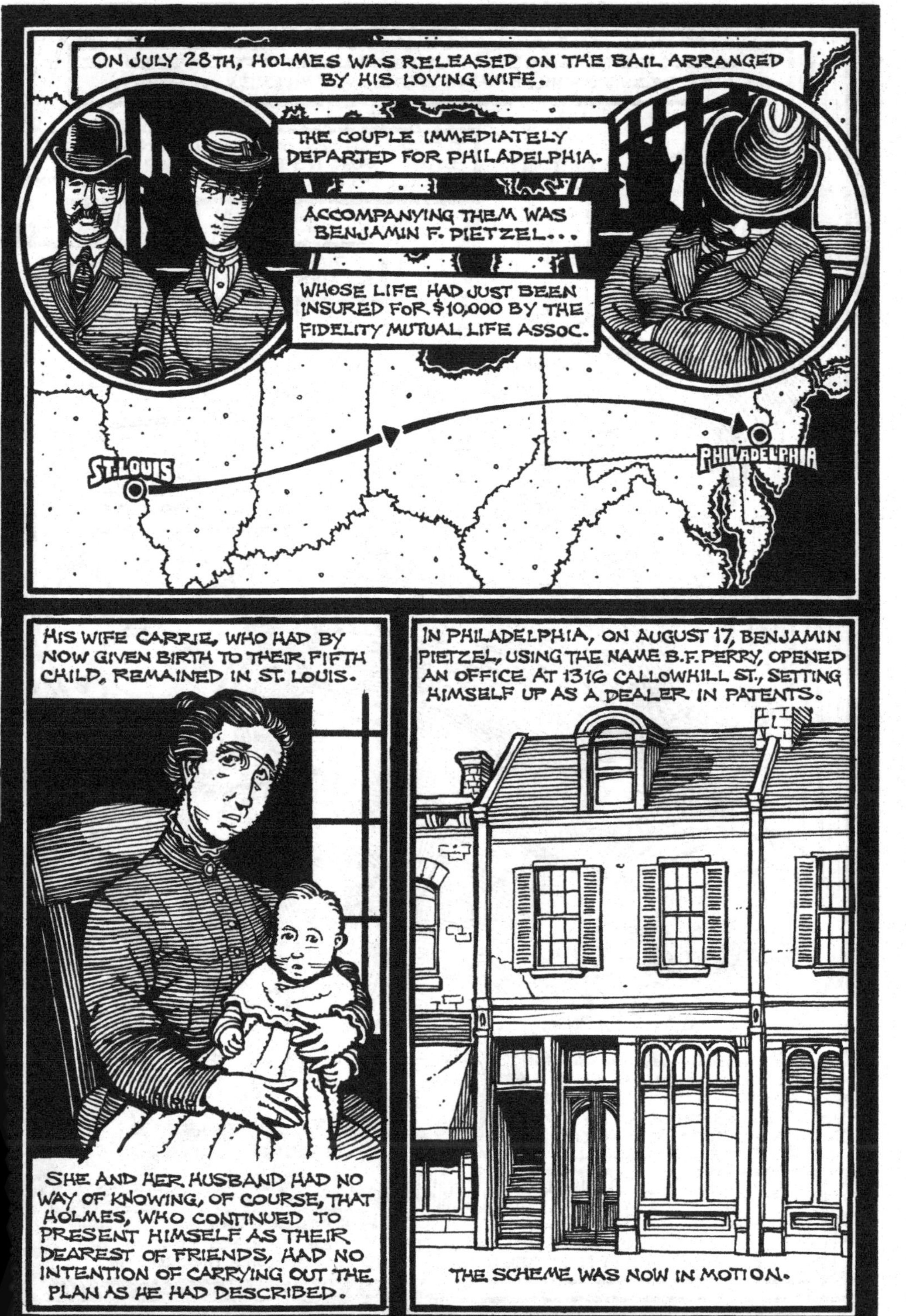
ON JULY 28TH, HOLMES WAS RELEASED ON THE BAIL ARRANGED BY HIS LOVING WIFE.
THE COUPLE IMMEDIATELY DEPARTED FOR PHILADELPHIA.
ACCOMPANYING THEM WAS BENJAMIN F. PIETZEL...
WHOSE LIFE HAD JUST BEEN INSURED FOR $10,000 BY THE FIDELITY MUTUAL LIFE ASSOC.
ST. LOUIS
PHILADELPHIA
HIS WIFE CARRIE, WHO HAD BY NOW GIVEN BIRTH TO THEIR FIFTH CHILD, REMAINED IN ST. LOUIS.
SHE AND HER HUSBAND HAD NO WAY OF KNOWING, OF COURSE, THAT HOLMES, WHO CONTINUED TO PRESENT HIMSELF AS THEIR DEAREST OF FRIENDS, HAD NO INTENTION OF CARRYING OUT THE PLAN AS HE HAD DESCRIBED.
IN PHILADELPHIA, ON AUGUST 17, BENJAMIN PIETZEL, USING THE NAME B.F. PERRY, OPENED AN OFFICE AT 1316 CALLOWHILL ST., SETTING HIMSELF UP AS A DEALER IN PATENTS.
THE SCHEME WAS NOW IN MOTION.

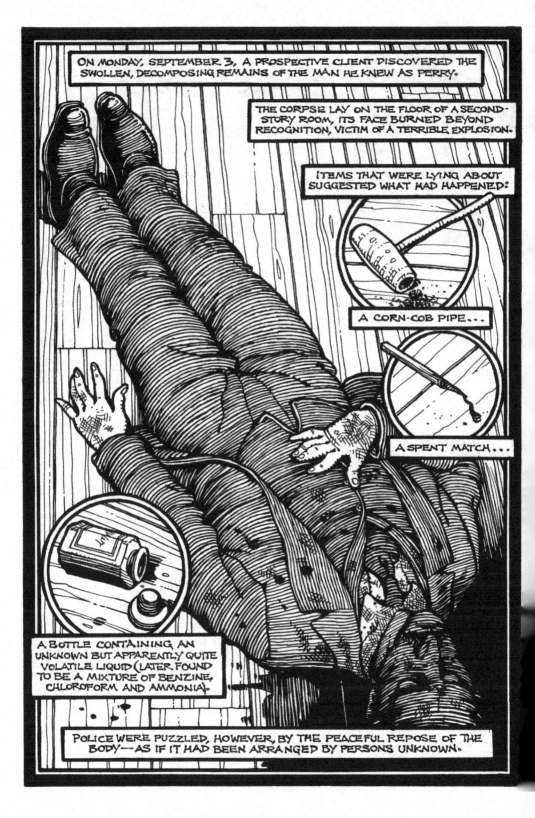

ON MONDAY, SEPTEMBER 3, A PROSPECTIVE CLIENT DISCOVERED THE SWOLLEN, DECOMPOSING REMAINS OF THE MAN HE KNEW AS PERRY.

THE CORPSE LAY ON THE FLOOR OF A SECOND-STORY ROOM, ITS FACE BURNED BEYOND RECOGNITION, VICTIM OF A TERRIBLE EXPLOSION.

ITEMS THAT WERE LYING ABOUT SUGGESTED WHAT HAD HAPPENED:

A CORN-COB PIPE...

A SPENT MATCH...

A BOTTLE CONTAINING AN UNKNOWN BUT APPARENTLY QUITE VOLATILE LIQUID (LATER FOUND TO BE A MIXTURE OF BENZINE, CHLOROFORM AND AMMONIA).

POLICE WERE PUZZLED, HOWEVER, BY THE PEACEFUL REPOSE OF THE BODY—AS IF IT HAD BEEN ARRANGED BY PERSONS UNKNOWN.

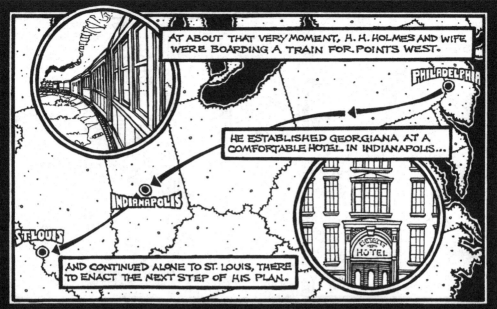

AT ABOUT THAT VERY MOMENT, H. H. HOLMES AND WIFE WERE BOARDING A TRAIN FOR POINTS WEST.

PHILADELPHIA

HE ESTABLISHED GEORGIANA AT A COMFORTABLE HOTEL IN INDIANAPOLIS...

INDIANAPOLIS

ST. LOUIS

HOTEL

AND CONTINUED ALONE TO ST. LOUIS, THERE TO ENACT THE NEXT STEP OF HIS PLAN.

IN THE MEANTIME, ON SEPTEMBER 5, AN INQUEST WAS CONDUCTED IN PHILADELPHIA OVER THE SAD REMAINS OF "B. F. PERRY."

NO RELATION CAME FORWARD TO CLAIM HIM.

THE JURY'S CONCLUSION — THAT HE HAD PERISHED OF CHLOROFORM POISONING — LEFT OPEN MANY QUESTIONS: ACCIDENT? SUICIDE? MURDER?

MANY AMONG THE POLICE FORCE CONTINUED TO BELIEVE HIM A VICTIM OF FOUL PLAY.

ONCE IN ST. LOUIS, HOLMES BROUGHT CARRIE PIETZEL TO THE OFFICE OF JEPTHA D. HOWE...

(THE ATTORNEY RECOMMENDED BY MARION HEDGEPETH).

A LETTER WAS COMPOSED TO THE FIDELITY MUTUAL LIFE ASSOC., CLAIMING $10,000 ON THE LIFE OF BENJAMIN F. PIETZEL.

IT WAS DECIDED THAT THE PIETZELS' 15-YEAR-OLD DAUGHTER ALICE WOULD ACCOMPANY HOWE TO PHILADELPHIA, TO "IDENTIFY" AND CLAIM THE REMAINS.

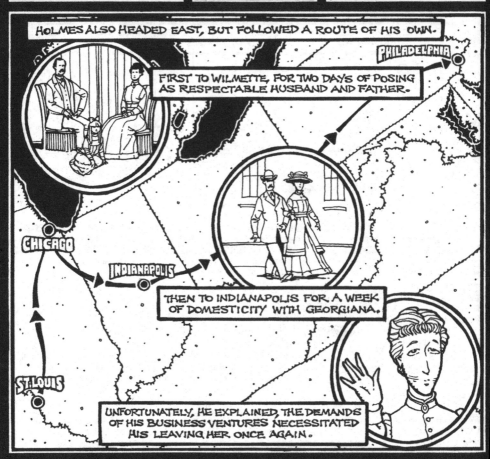

HOLMES ALSO HEADED EAST, BUT FOLLOWED A ROUTE OF HIS OWN.

PHILADELPHIA

FIRST TO WILMETTE, FOR TWO DAYS OF POSING AS RESPECTABLE HUSBAND AND FATHER.

CHICAGO

INDIANAPOLIS

THEN TO INDIANAPOLIS FOR A WEEK OF DOMESTICITY WITH GEORGIANA.

ST. LOUIS

UNFORTUNATELY, HE EXPLAINED, THE DEMANDS OF HIS BUSINESS VENTURES NECESSITATED HIS LEAVING HER ONCE AGAIN.

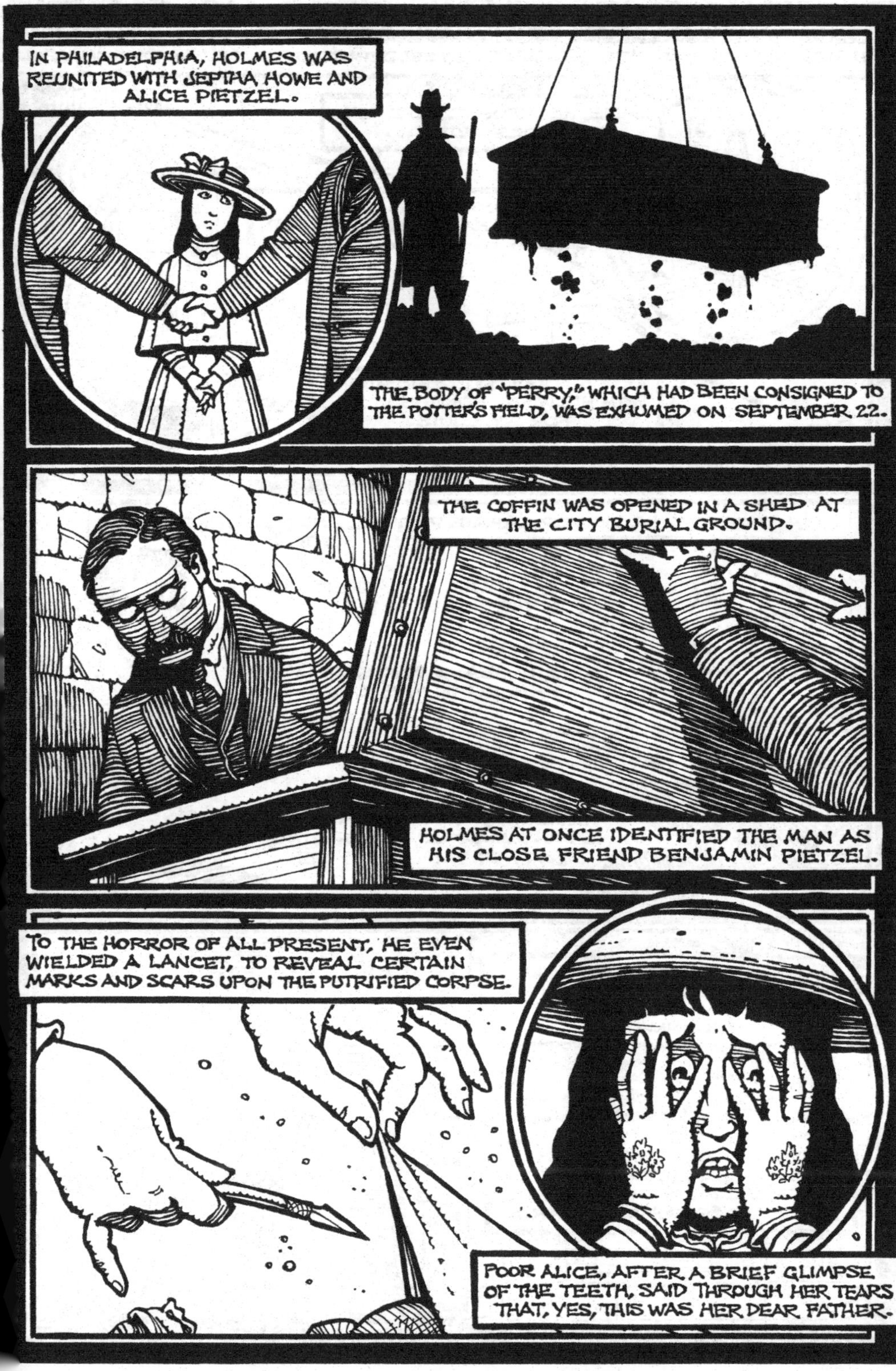
IN PHILADELPHIA, HOLMES WAS REUNITED WITH JEPTHA HOWE AND ALICE PIETZEL.
THE BODY OF "PERRY," WHICH HAD BEEN CONSIGNED TO THE POTTER'S FIELD, WAS EXHUMED ON SEPTEMBER 22.
THE COFFIN WAS OPENED IN A SHED AT THE CITY BURIAL GROUND.
HOLMES AT ONCE IDENTIFIED THE MAN AS HIS CLOSE FRIEND BENJAMIN PIETZEL.
TO THE HORROR OF ALL PRESENT, HE EVEN WIELDED A LANCET, TO REVEAL CERTAIN MARKS AND SCARS UPON THE PUTRIFIED CORPSE.
POOR ALICE, AFTER A BRIEF GLIMPSE OF THE TEETH, SAID THROUGH HER TEARS THAT, YES, THIS WAS HER DEAR FATHER.

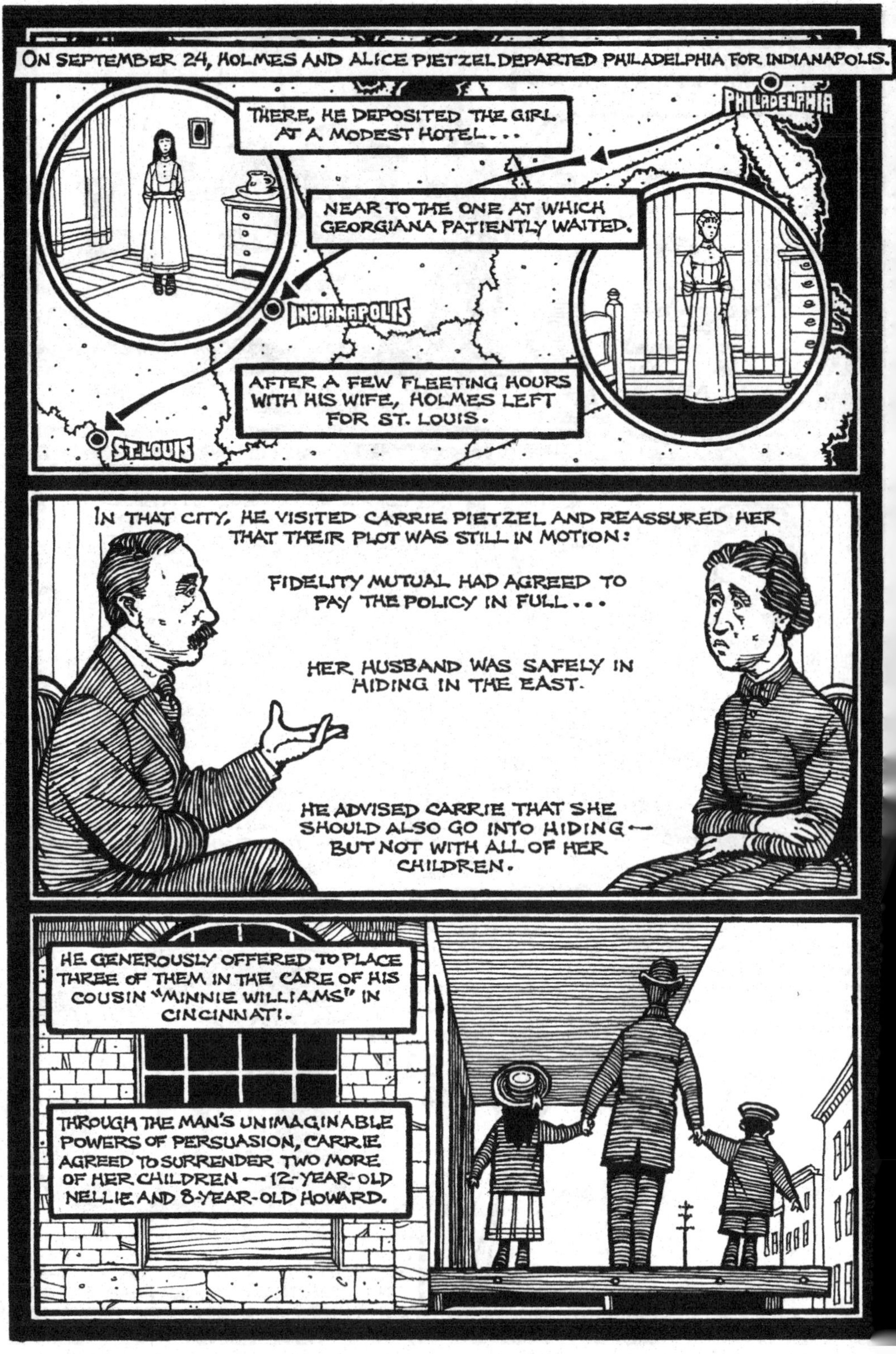

ON SEPTEMBER 24, HOLMES AND ALICE PIETZEL DEPARTED PHILADELPHIA FOR INDIANAPOLIS.
PHILADELPHIA
THERE, HE DEPOSITED THE GIRL AT A MODEST HOTEL...
NEAR TO THE ONE AT WHICH GEORGIANA PATIENTLY WAITED.
INDIANAPOLIS
AFTER A FEW FLEETING HOURS WITH HIS WIFE, HOLMES LEFT FOR ST. LOUIS.
ST. LOUIS
IN THAT CITY, HE VISITED CARRIE PIETZEL AND REASSURED HER THAT THEIR PLOT WAS STILL IN MOTION:
FIDELITY MUTUAL HAD AGREED TO PAY THE POLICY IN FULL...
HER HUSBAND WAS SAFELY IN HIDING IN THE EAST.
HE ADVISED CARRIE THAT SHE SHOULD ALSO GO INTO HIDING— BUT NOT WITH ALL OF HER CHILDREN.
HE GENEROUSLY OFFERED TO PLACE THREE OF THEM IN THE CARE OF HIS COUSIN "MINNIE WILLIAMS" IN CINCINNATI.
THROUGH THE MAN'S UNIMAGINABLE POWERS OF PERSUASION, CARRIE AGREED TO SURRENDER TWO MORE OF HER CHILDREN — 12-YEAR-OLD NELLIE AND 8-YEAR-OLD HOWARD.

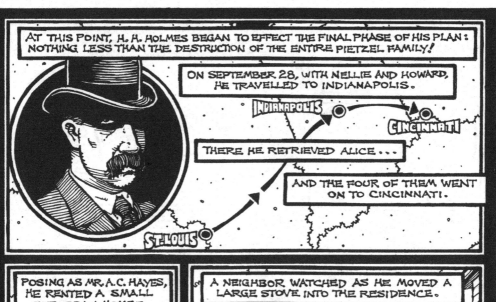

AT THIS POINT, H. H. HOLMES BEGAN TO EFFECT THE FINAL PHASE OF HIS PLAN: NOTHING LESS THAN THE DESTRUCTION OF THE ENTIRE PIETZEL FAMILY!

ON SEPTEMBER 28, WITH NELLIE AND HOWARD, HE TRAVELLED TO INDIANAPOLIS.

INDIANAPOLIS

CINCINNATI

THERE HE RETRIEVED ALICE...

AND THE FOUR OF THEM WENT ON TO CINCINNATI.

ST. LOUIS

POSING AS MR. A.C. HAYES, HE RENTED A SMALL SUBURBAN HOUSE.

305 POPLAR STREET

A NEIGHBOR WATCHED AS HE MOVED A LARGE STOVE INTO THE RESIDENCE.

WHATEVER WAS AFOOT, HOWEVER, HAD TO BE ABANDONED, AND HOLMES RETURNED WITH THE THREE CHILDREN TO INDIANAPOLIS.

APOLIS

CINCI

HE RESETTLED THEM INTO ANOTHER SMALL HOTEL, CLOSE TO THE ONE WHERE HIS WIFE REMAINED.

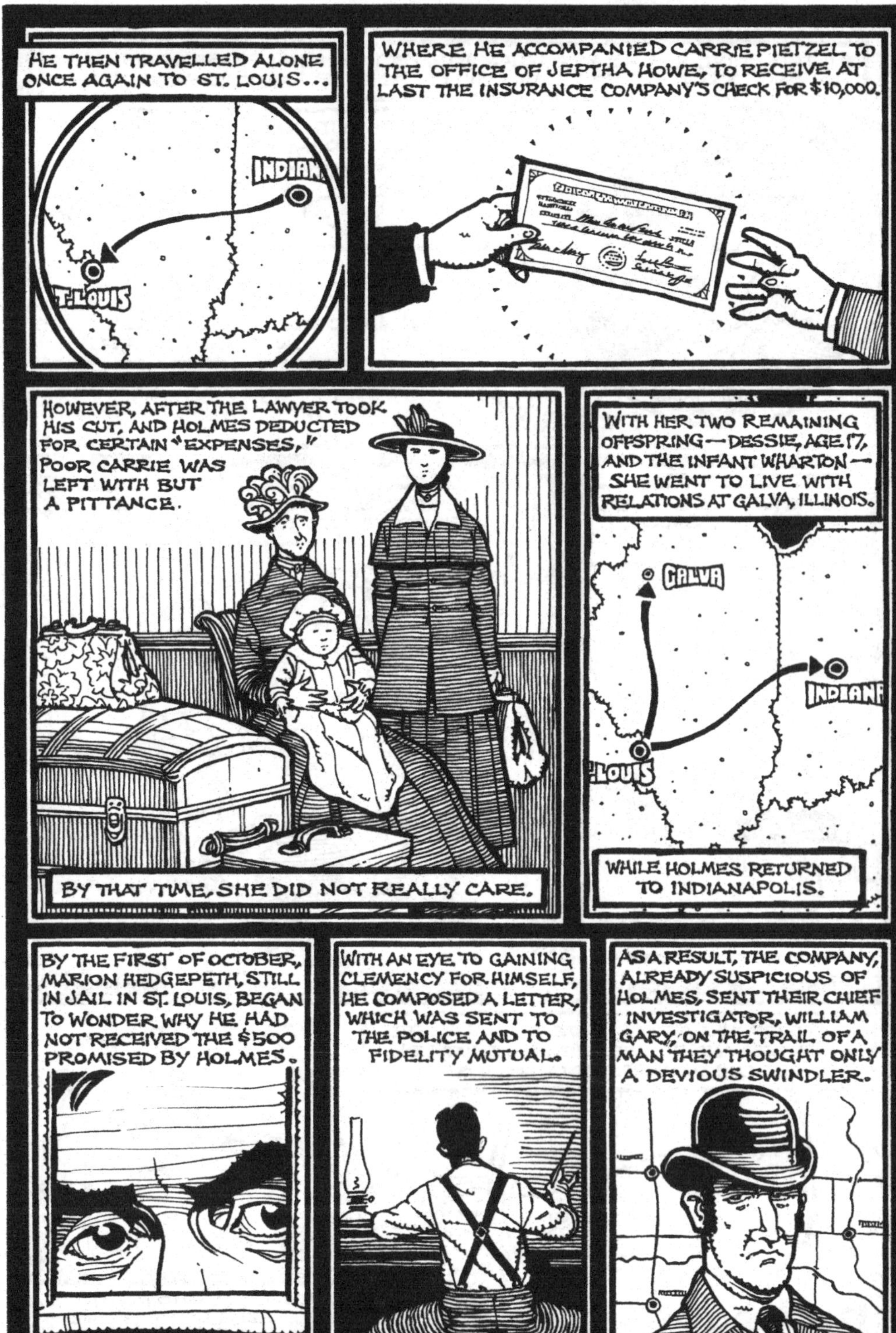
HE THEN TRAVELLED ALONE ONCE AGAIN TO ST. LOUIS...
INDIAN
ST. LOUIS
WHERE HE ACCOMPANIED CARRIE PIETZEL TO THE OFFICE OF JEPTHA HOWE, TO RECEIVE AT LAST THE INSURANCE COMPANY'S CHECK FOR $10,000.
HOWEVER, AFTER THE LAWYER TOOK HIS CUT, AND HOLMES DEDUCTED FOR CERTAIN "EXPENSES," POOR CARRIE WAS LEFT WITH BUT A PITTANCE.
BY THAT TIME, SHE DID NOT REALLY CARE.
WITH HER TWO REMAINING OFFSPRING — DESSIE, AGE 17, AND THE INFANT WHARTON — SHE WENT TO LIVE WITH RELATIONS AT GALVA, ILLINOIS.
GALVA
INDIANA
LOUIS
WHILE HOLMES RETURNED TO INDIANAPOLIS.
BY THE FIRST OF OCTOBER, MARION HEDGEPETH, STILL IN JAIL IN ST. LOUIS, BEGAN TO WONDER WHY HE HAD NOT RECEIVED THE $500 PROMISED BY HOLMES.
WITH AN EYE TO GAINING CLEMENCY FOR HIMSELF, HE COMPOSED A LETTER, WHICH WAS SENT TO THE POLICE AND TO FIDELITY MUTUAL.
AS A RESULT, THE COMPANY, ALREADY SUSPICIOUS OF HOLMES, SENT THEIR CHIEF INVESTIGATOR, WILLIAM GARY, ON THE TRAIL OF A MAN THEY THOUGHT ONLY A DEVIOUS SWINDLER.

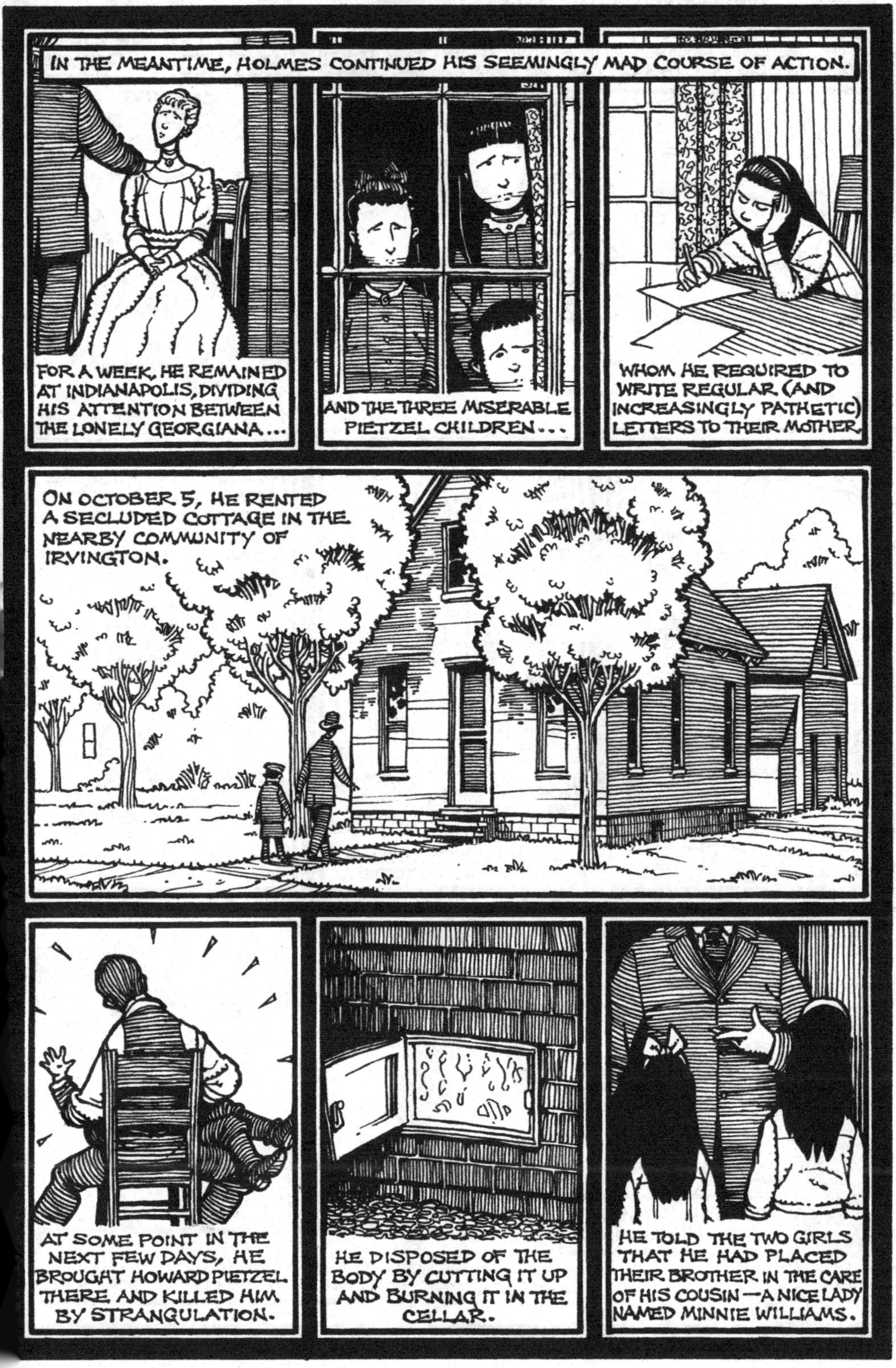
IN THE MEANTIME, HOLMES CONTINUED HIS SEEMINGLY MAD COURSE OF ACTION.
FOR A WEEK, HE REMAINED AT INDIANAPOLIS, DIVIDING HIS ATTENTION BETWEEN THE LONELY GEORGIANA...
AND THE THREE MISERABLE PIETZEL CHILDREN...
WHOM HE REQUIRED TO WRITE REGULAR (AND INCREASINGLY PATHETIC) LETTERS TO THEIR MOTHER.
ON OCTOBER 5, HE RENTED A SECLUDED COTTAGE IN THE NEARBY COMMUNITY OF IRVINGTON.
AT SOME POINT IN THE NEXT FEW DAYS, HE BROUGHT HOWARD PIETZEL THERE AND KILLED HIM BY STRANGULATION.
HE DISPOSED OF THE BODY BY CUTTING IT UP AND BURNING IT IN THE CELLAR.
HE TOLD THE TWO GIRLS THAT HE HAD PLACED THEIR BROTHER IN THE CARE OF HIS COUSIN—A NICE LADY NAMED MINNIE WILLIAMS.

ON OCTOBER 12, HOLMES AND HIS WIFE LEFT INDIANAPOLIS FOR THE CITY OF DETROIT.

DETROIT

IN A SEPARATE COACH, UNBEKNOWNST TO GEORGIANA, WERE ALICE AND NELLIE PIETZEL.

INDIANAPOLIS

HE SETTLED THE GIRLS AT A HOTEL, UNDER THE NAMES ETTA AND NELLIE CANNING...

WHILE HE AND GEORGIANA REGISTERED AT A NEARBY ESTABLISHMENT AS G. HOWELL AND WIFE ADRIAN.

HOTEL.

TWO DAYS LATER, CARRIE PIETZEL, WITH DESSIE AND WHARTON, ARRIVED ON AN URGENT SUMMONS FROM HOLMES TO AT LAST MEET HER HUSBAND.

HE ENSCONCED THEM AT YET A THIRD HOTEL.

HE SOON INFORMED THE DISTRAUGHT CARRIE THAT ALICE, NELLIE AND HOWARD HAD REMAINED AT INDIANAPOLIS AND THAT HER HUSBAND HAD MOVED ON TO TORONTO.

THE FAMILY WOULD HAVE ITS REUNION IN CANADA!

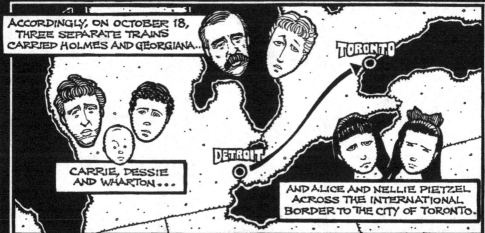

ACCORDINGLY, ON OCTOBER 18, THREE SEPARATE TRAINS CARRIED HOLMES AND GEORGIANA...

TORONTO

CARRIE, DESSIE AND WHARTON...

DETROIT

AND ALICE AND NELLIE PIETZEL ACROSS THE INTERNATIONAL BORDER TO THE CITY OF TORONTO.

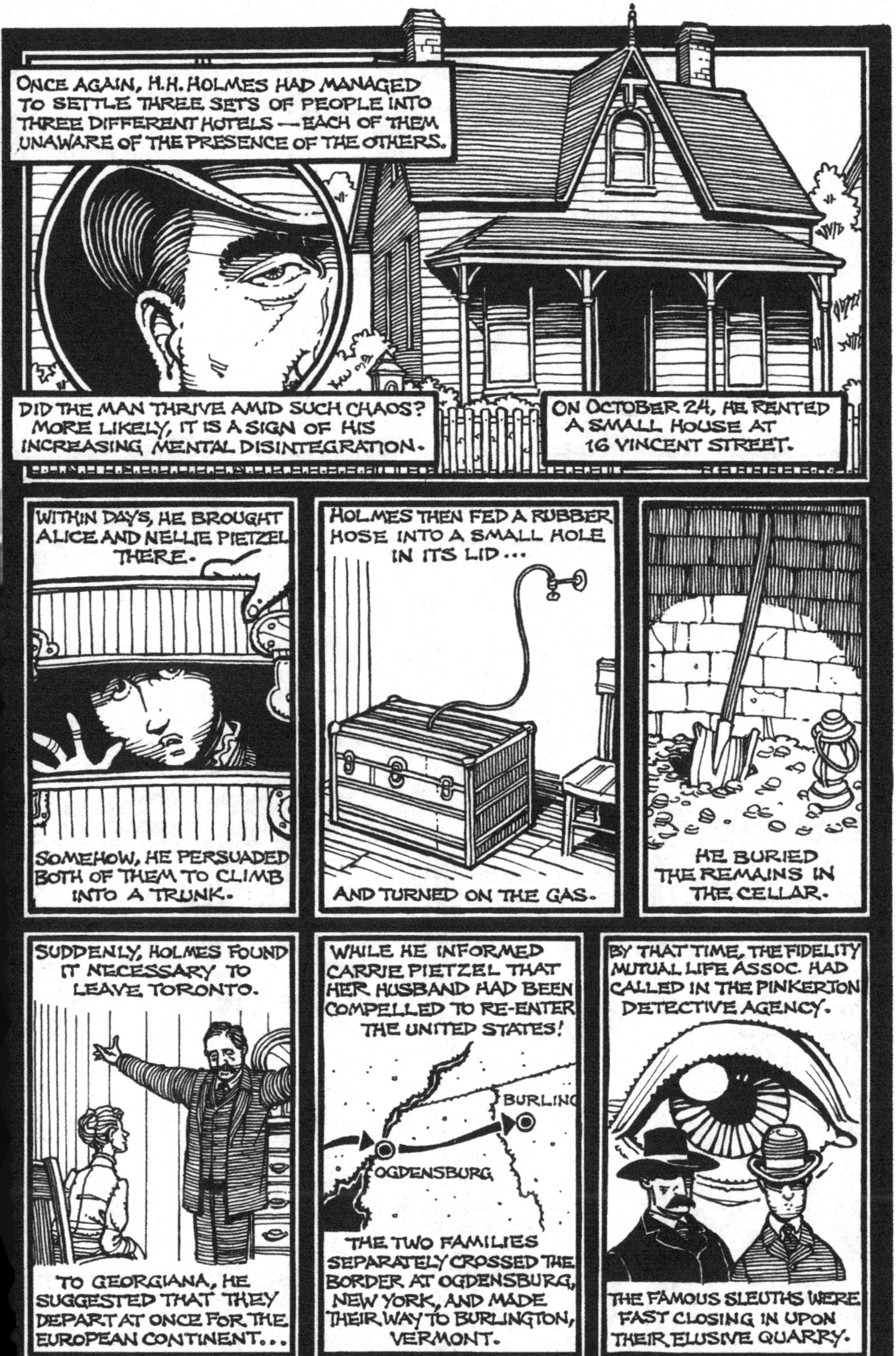
ONCE AGAIN, H.H. HOLMES HAD MANAGED TO SETTLE THREE SETS OF PEOPLE INTO THREE DIFFERENT HOTELS — EACH OF THEM UNAWARE OF THE PRESENCE OF THE OTHERS.
DID THE MAN THRIVE AMID SUCH CHAOS? MORE LIKELY, IT IS A SIGN OF HIS INCREASING MENTAL DISINTEGRATION.
ON OCTOBER 24, HE RENTED A SMALL HOUSE AT 16 VINCENT STREET.
WITHIN DAYS, HE BROUGHT ALICE AND NELLIE PIETZEL THERE.
SOMEHOW, HE PERSUADED BOTH OF THEM TO CLIMB INTO A TRUNK.
HOLMES THEN FED A RUBBER HOSE INTO A SMALL HOLE IN ITS LID...
AND TURNED ON THE GAS.
HE BURIED THE REMAINS IN THE CELLAR.
SUDDENLY, HOLMES FOUND IT NECESSARY TO LEAVE TORONTO.
TO GEORGIANA, HE SUGGESTED THAT THEY DEPART AT ONCE FOR THE EUROPEAN CONTINENT...
WHILE HE INFORMED CARRIE PIETZEL THAT HER HUSBAND HAD BEEN COMPELLED TO RE-ENTER THE UNITED STATES!
BURLING
OGDENSBURG
THE TWO FAMILIES SEPARATELY CROSSED THE BORDER AT OGDENSBURG, NEW YORK, AND MADE THEIR WAY TO BURLINGTON, VERMONT.
BY THAT TIME, THE FIDELITY MUTUAL LIFE ASSOC. HAD CALLED IN THE PINKERTON DETECTIVE AGENCY.
THE FAMOUS SLEUTHS WERE FAST CLOSING IN UPON THEIR ELUSIVE QUARRY.

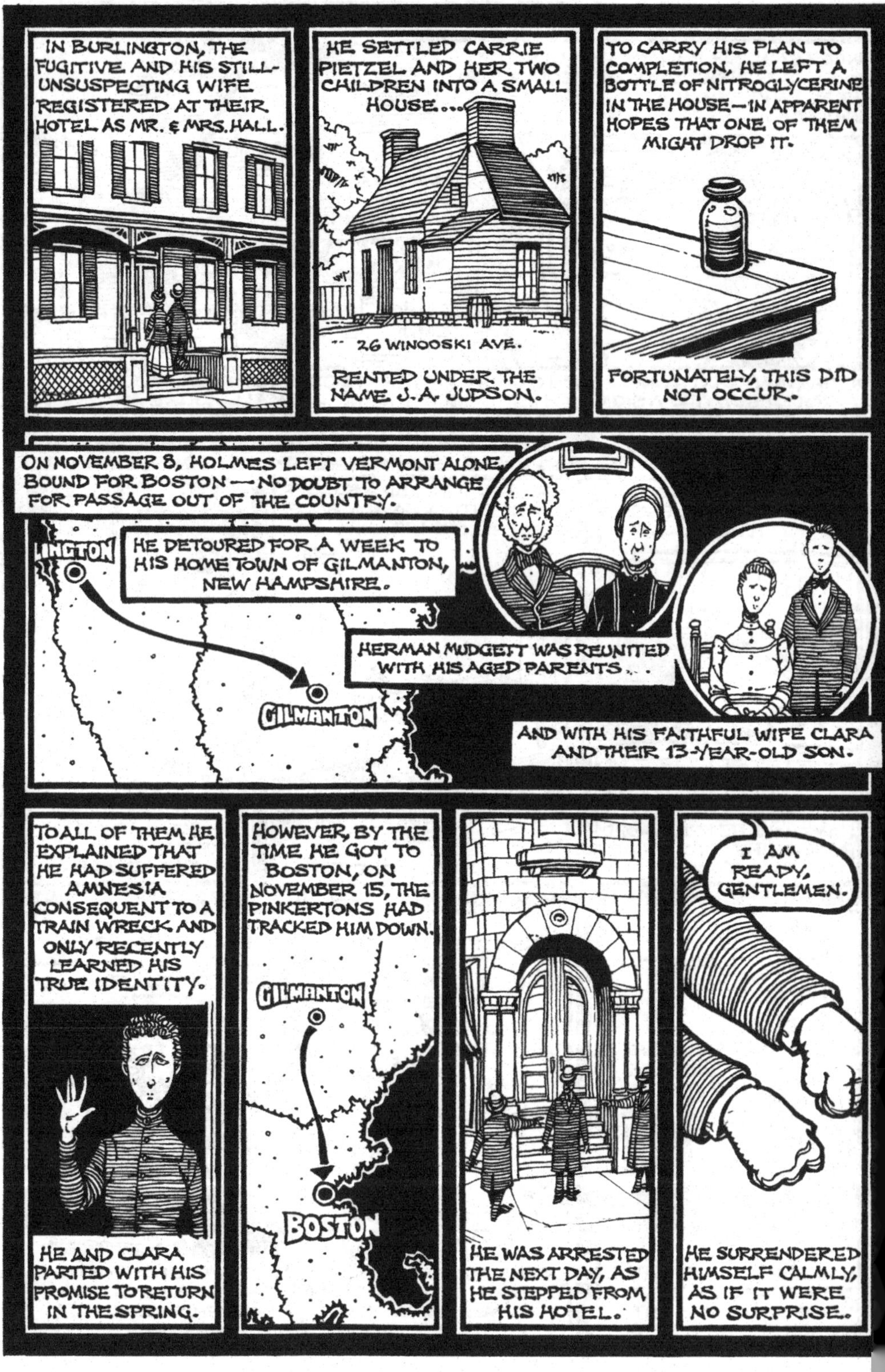
IN BURLINGTON, THE FUGITIVE AND HIS STILL-UNSUSPECTING WIFE REGISTERED AT THEIR HOTEL AS MR. & MRS. HALL.
HE SETTLED CARRIE PIETZEL AND HER TWO CHILDREN INTO A SMALL HOUSE....
26 WINOOSKI AVE.
RENTED UNDER THE NAME J. A. JUDSON.
TO CARRY HIS PLAN TO COMPLETION, HE LEFT A BOTTLE OF NITROGLYCERINE IN THE HOUSE—IN APPARENT HOPES THAT ONE OF THEM MIGHT DROP IT.
FORTUNATELY, THIS DID NOT OCCUR.
ON NOVEMBER 8, HOLMES LEFT VERMONT ALONE, BOUND FOR BOSTON — NO DOUBT TO ARRANGE FOR PASSAGE OUT OF THE COUNTRY.
LINGTON
HE DETOURED FOR A WEEK TO HIS HOME TOWN OF GILMANTON, NEW HAMPSHIRE.
GILMANTON
HERMAN MUDGETT WAS REUNITED WITH HIS AGED PARENTS...
AND WITH HIS FAITHFUL WIFE CLARA AND THEIR 13-YEAR-OLD SON.
TO ALL OF THEM HE EXPLAINED THAT HE HAD SUFFERED AMNESIA CONSEQUENT TO A TRAIN WRECK AND ONLY RECENTLY LEARNED HIS TRUE IDENTITY.
HE AND CLARA PARTED WITH HIS PROMISE TO RETURN IN THE SPRING.
HOWEVER, BY THE TIME HE GOT TO BOSTON, ON NOVEMBER 15, THE PINKERTONS HAD TRACKED HIM DOWN.
GILMANTON
BOSTON
HE WAS ARRESTED THE NEXT DAY, AS HE STEPPED FROM HIS HOTEL.
I AM READY, GENTLEMEN.
HE SURRENDERED HIMSELF CALMLY, AS IF IT WERE NO SURPRISE.

PART IV.

THE CASTLE REVEALED

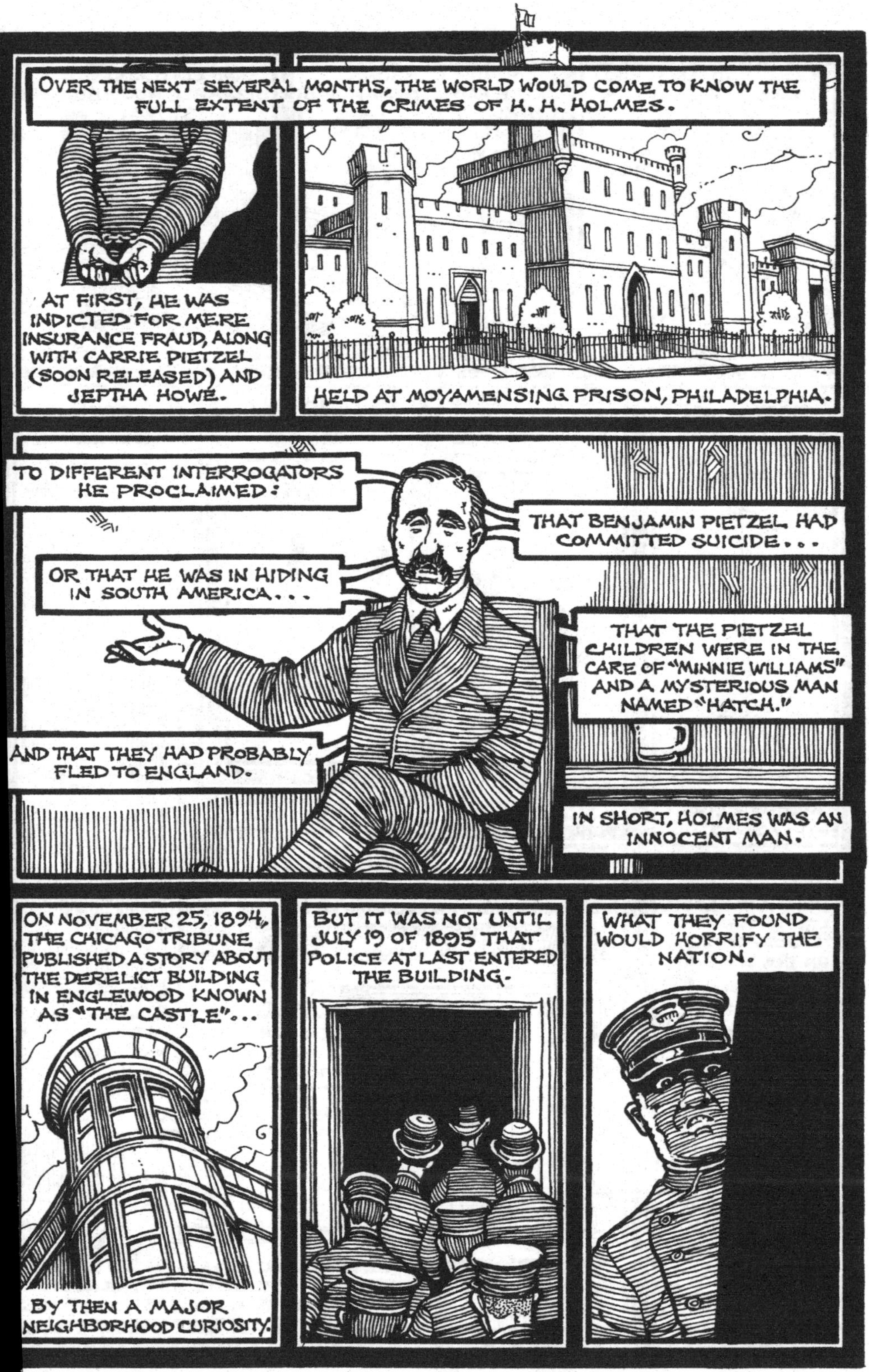

AT FIRST, HE WAS INDICTED FOR MERE INSURANCE FRAUD, ALONG WITH CARRIE PIETZEL (SOON RELEASED) AND JEPTHA HOWE.
OVER THE NEXT SEVERAL MONTHS, THE WORLD WOULD COME TO KNOW THE FULL EXTENT OF THE CRIMES OF H. H. HOLMES.
HELD AT MOYAMENSING PRISON, PHILADELPHIA.
TO DIFFERENT INTERROGATORS HE PROCLAIMED:
THAT BENJAMIN PIETZEL HAD COMMITTED SUICIDE...
OR THAT HE WAS IN HIDING IN SOUTH AMERICA...
THAT THE PIETZEL CHILDREN WERE IN THE CARE OF "MINNIE WILLIAMS" AND A MYSTERIOUS MAN NAMED "HATCH."
AND THAT THEY HAD PROBABLY FLED TO ENGLAND.
IN SHORT, HOLMES WAS AN INNOCENT MAN.
ON NOVEMBER 25, 1894, THE CHICAGO TRIBUNE PUBLISHED A STORY ABOUT THE DERELICT BUILDING IN ENGLEWOOD KNOWN AS "THE CASTLE"...
BY THEN A MAJOR NEIGHBORHOOD CURIOSITY.
BUT IT WAS NOT UNTIL JULY 19 OF 1895 THAT POLICE AT LAST ENTERED THE BUILDING.
WHAT THEY FOUND WOULD HORRIFY THE NATION.

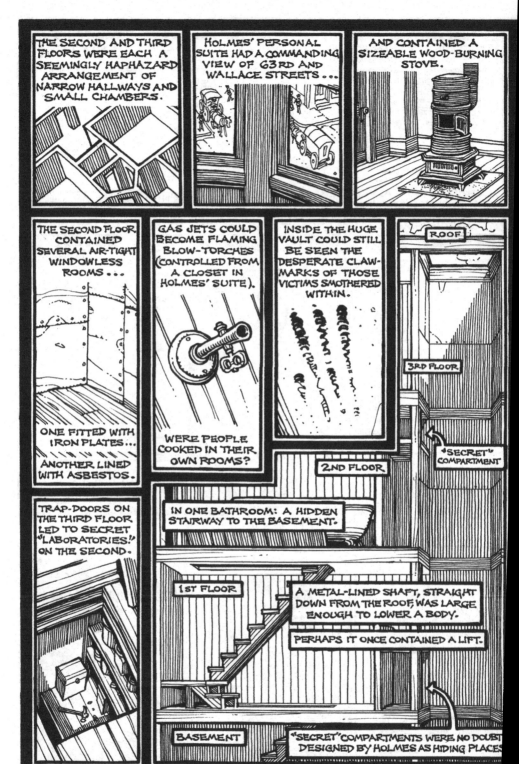

THE SECOND AND THIRD FLOORS WERE EACH A SEEMINGLY HAPHAZARD ARRANGEMENT OF NARROW HALLWAYS AND SMALL CHAMBERS.

HOLMES' PERSONAL SUITE HAD A COMMANDING VIEW OF 63RD AND WALLACE STREETS...

AND CONTAINED A SIZEABLE WOOD-BURNING STOVE.

THE SECOND FLOOR CONTAINED SEVERAL AIR-TIGHT WINDOWLESS ROOMS...

ONE FITTED WITH IRON PLATES... ANOTHER LINED WITH ASBESTOS.

GAS JETS COULD BECOME FLAMING BLOW-TORCHES (CONTROLLED FROM A CLOSET IN HOLMES' SUITE).

WERE PEOPLE COOKED IN THEIR OWN ROOMS?

INSIDE THE HUGE VAULT COULD STILL BE SEEN THE DESPERATE CLAW-MARKS OF THOSE VICTIMS SMOTHERED WITHIN.

ROOF

3RD FLOOR

"SECRET" COMPARTMENT

2ND FLOOR

TRAP-DOORS ON THE THIRD FLOOR LED TO SECRET "LABORATORIES!" ON THE SECOND.

IN ONE BATHROOM: A HIDDEN STAIRWAY TO THE BASEMENT.

1ST FLOOR

A METAL-LINED SHAFT, STRAIGHT DOWN FROM THE ROOF, WAS LARGE ENOUGH TO LOWER A BODY.

PERHAPS IT ONCE CONTAINED A LIFT.

BASEMENT

"SECRET" COMPARTMENTS WERE NO DOUBT DESIGNED BY HOLMES AS HIDING PLACES

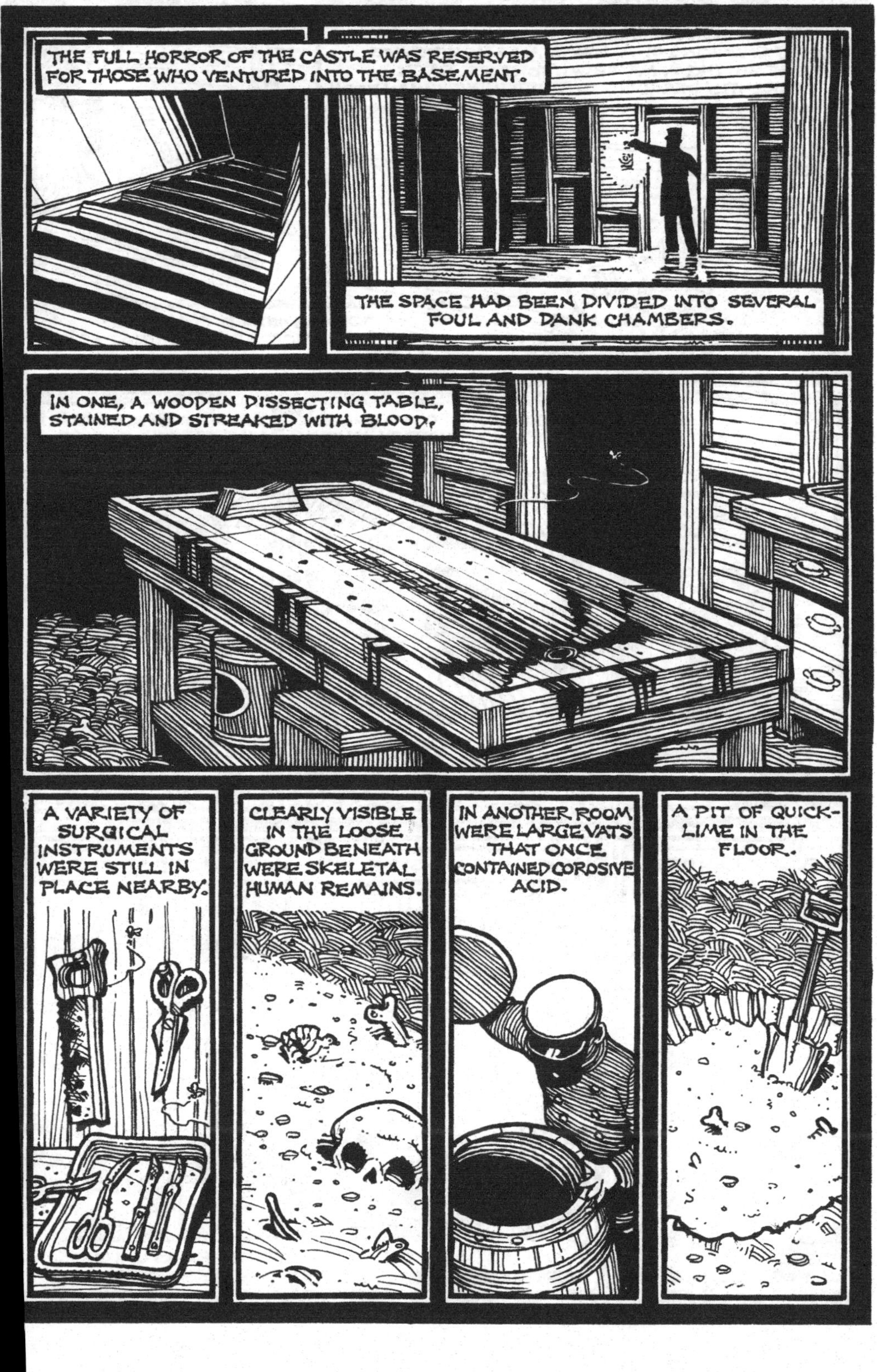
THE FULL HORROR OF THE CASTLE WAS RESERVED FOR THOSE WHO VENTURED INTO THE BASEMENT.
THE SPACE HAD BEEN DIVIDED INTO SEVERAL FOUL AND DANK CHAMBERS.
IN ONE, A WOODEN DISSECTING TABLE, STAINED AND STREAKED WITH BLOOD.
A VARIETY OF SURGICAL INSTRUMENTS WERE STILL IN PLACE NEARBY.
CLEARLY VISIBLE IN THE LOOSE GROUND BENEATH WERE SKELETAL HUMAN REMAINS.
IN ANOTHER ROOM WERE LARGE VATS THAT ONCE CONTAINED COROSIVE ACID.
A PIT OF QUICK-LIME IN THE FLOOR.

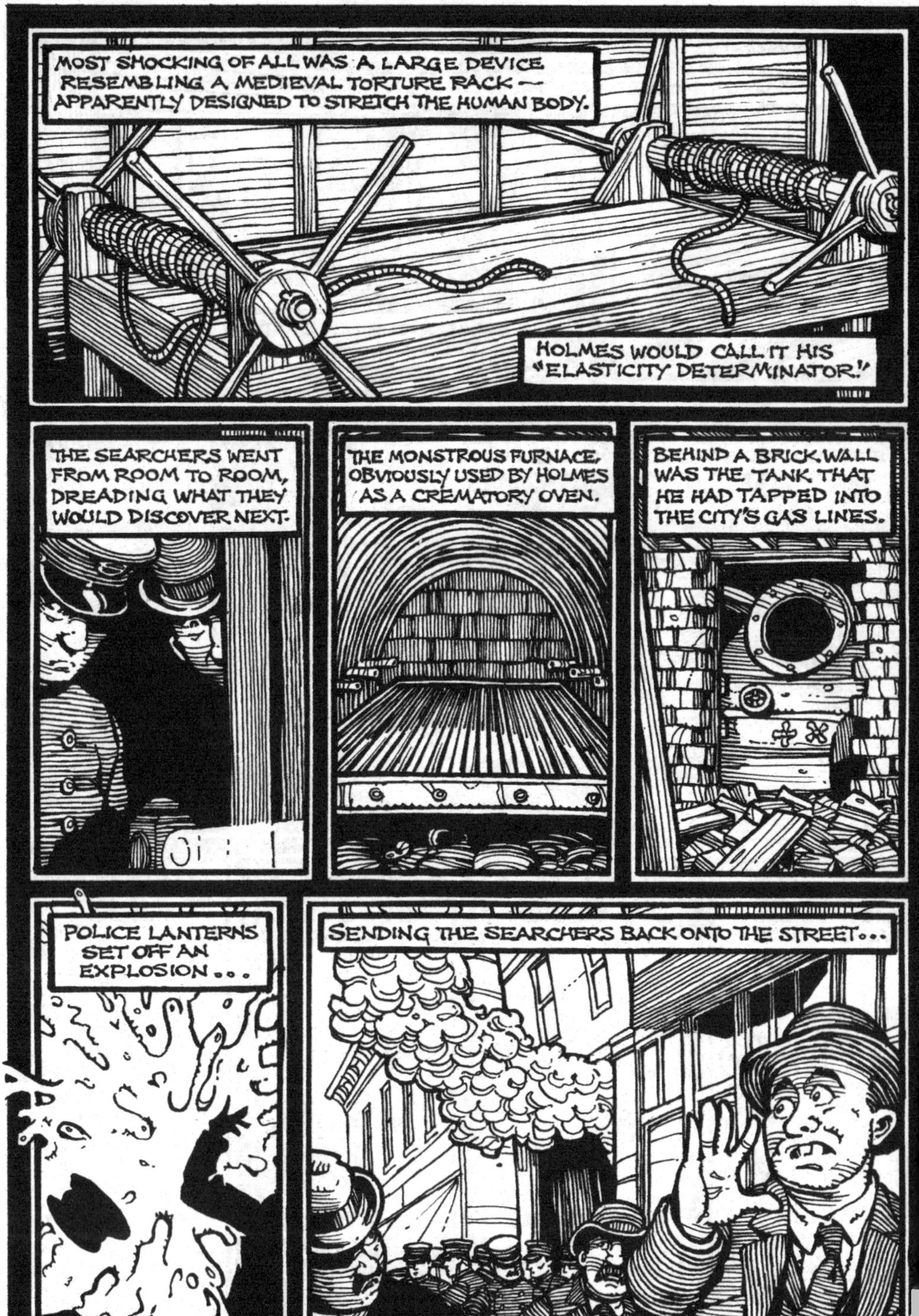
MOST SHOCKING OF ALL WAS A LARGE DEVICE RESEMBLING A MEDIEVAL TORTURE RACK — APPARENTLY DESIGNED TO STRETCH THE HUMAN BODY.
HOLMES WOULD CALL IT HIS "ELASTICITY DETERMINATOR."
THE SEARCHERS WENT FROM ROOM TO ROOM, DREADING WHAT THEY WOULD DISCOVER NEXT.
THE MONSTROUS FURNACE, OBVIOUSLY USED BY HOLMES AS A CREMATORY OVEN.
BEHIND A BRICK WALL WAS THE TANK THAT HE HAD TAPPED INTO THE CITY'S GAS LINES.
POLICE LANTERNS SET OFF AN EXPLOSION . . .
SENDING THE SEARCHERS BACK ONTO THE STREET . . .
WHICH WAS BY THEN FILLED WITH CURIOUS ONLOOKERS.

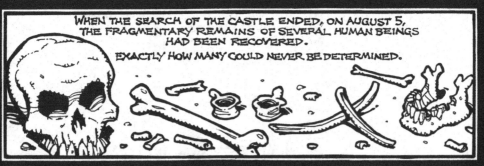

WHEN THE SEARCH OF THE CASTLE ENDED, ON AUGUST 5, THE FRAGMENTARY REMAINS OF SEVERAL HUMAN BEINGS HAD BEEN RECOVERED.

EXACTLY HOW MANY COULD NEVER BE DETERMINED.

ALSO, AN ARRAY OF PATHETIC RELICS: WATCHES, RINGS, BUTTONS, ETC.

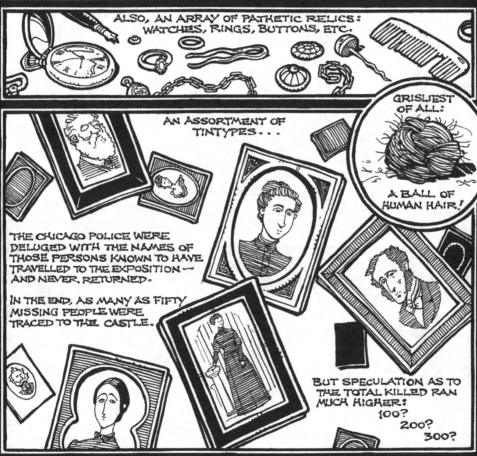

AN ASSORTMENT OF TINTYPES...

GRISLIEST OF ALL:

A BALL OF HUMAN HAIR!

THE CHICAGO POLICE WERE DELUGED WITH THE NAMES OF THOSE PERSONS KNOWN TO HAVE TRAVELLED TO THE EXPOSITION — AND NEVER RETURNED.

IN THE END, AS MANY AS FIFTY MISSING PEOPLE WERE TRACED TO THE CASTLE.

BUT SPECULATION AS TO THE TOTAL KILLED RAN MUCH HIGHER:
100?
200?
300?

THE GREAT CITY OF CHICAGO ONLY ENLARGED ITS REPUTATION AS "SLAUGHTER-HOUSE TO THE WORLD."

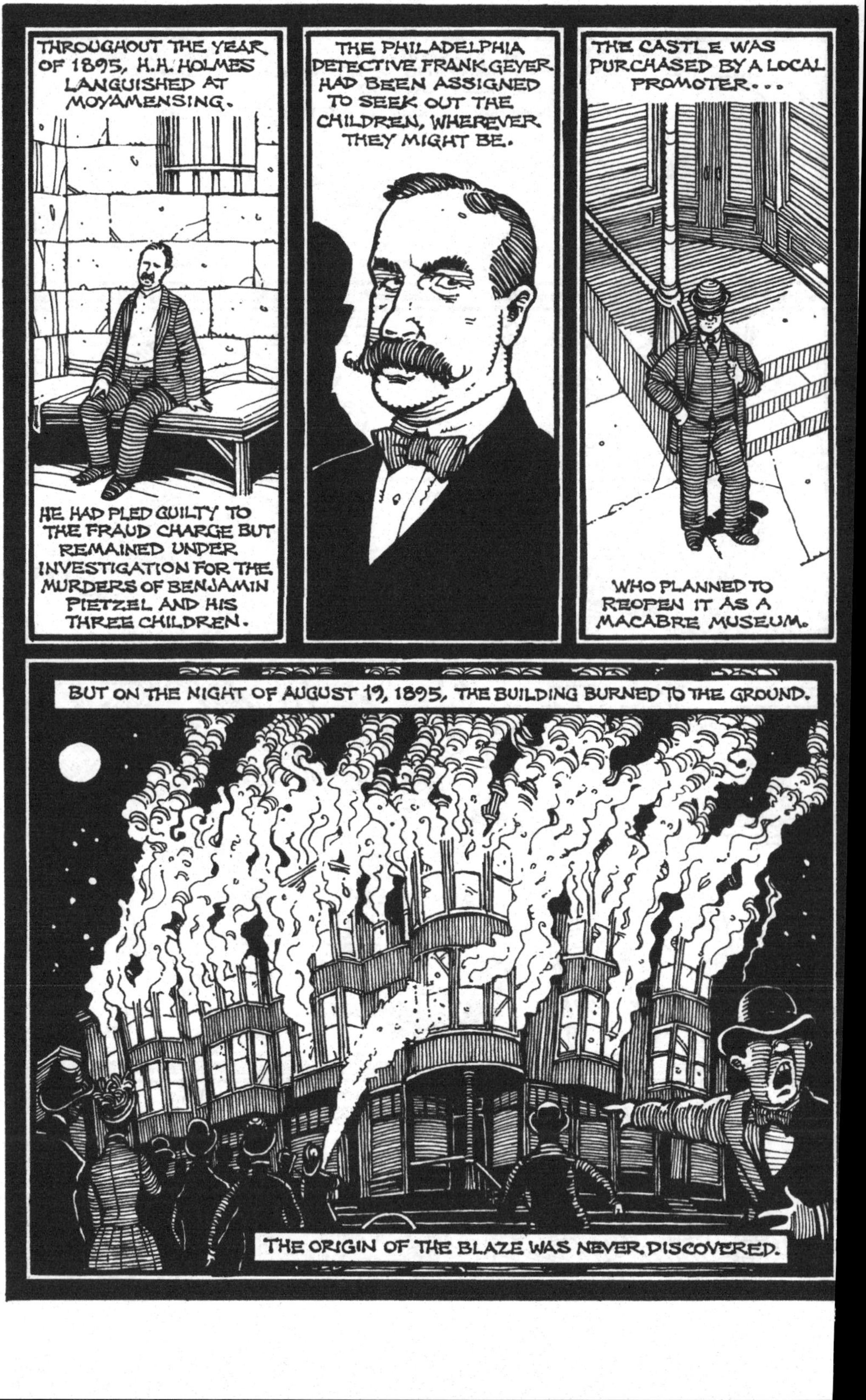
THROUGHOUT THE YEAR OF 1895, H.H. HOLMES LANGUISHED AT MOYAMENSING.
HE HAD PLED GUILTY TO THE FRAUD CHARGE BUT REMAINED UNDER INVESTIGATION FOR THE MURDERS OF BENJAMIN PIETZEL AND HIS THREE CHILDREN.
THE PHILADELPHIA DETECTIVE FRANK GEYER HAD BEEN ASSIGNED TO SEEK OUT THE CHILDREN, WHEREVER THEY MIGHT BE.
THE CASTLE WAS PURCHASED BY A LOCAL PROMOTER...
WHO PLANNED TO REOPEN IT AS A MACABRE MUSEUM.
BUT ON THE NIGHT OF AUGUST 19, 1895, THE BUILDING BURNED TO THE GROUND.
THE ORIGIN OF THE BLAZE WAS NEVER DISCOVERED.

PART V.
THE PRISONER

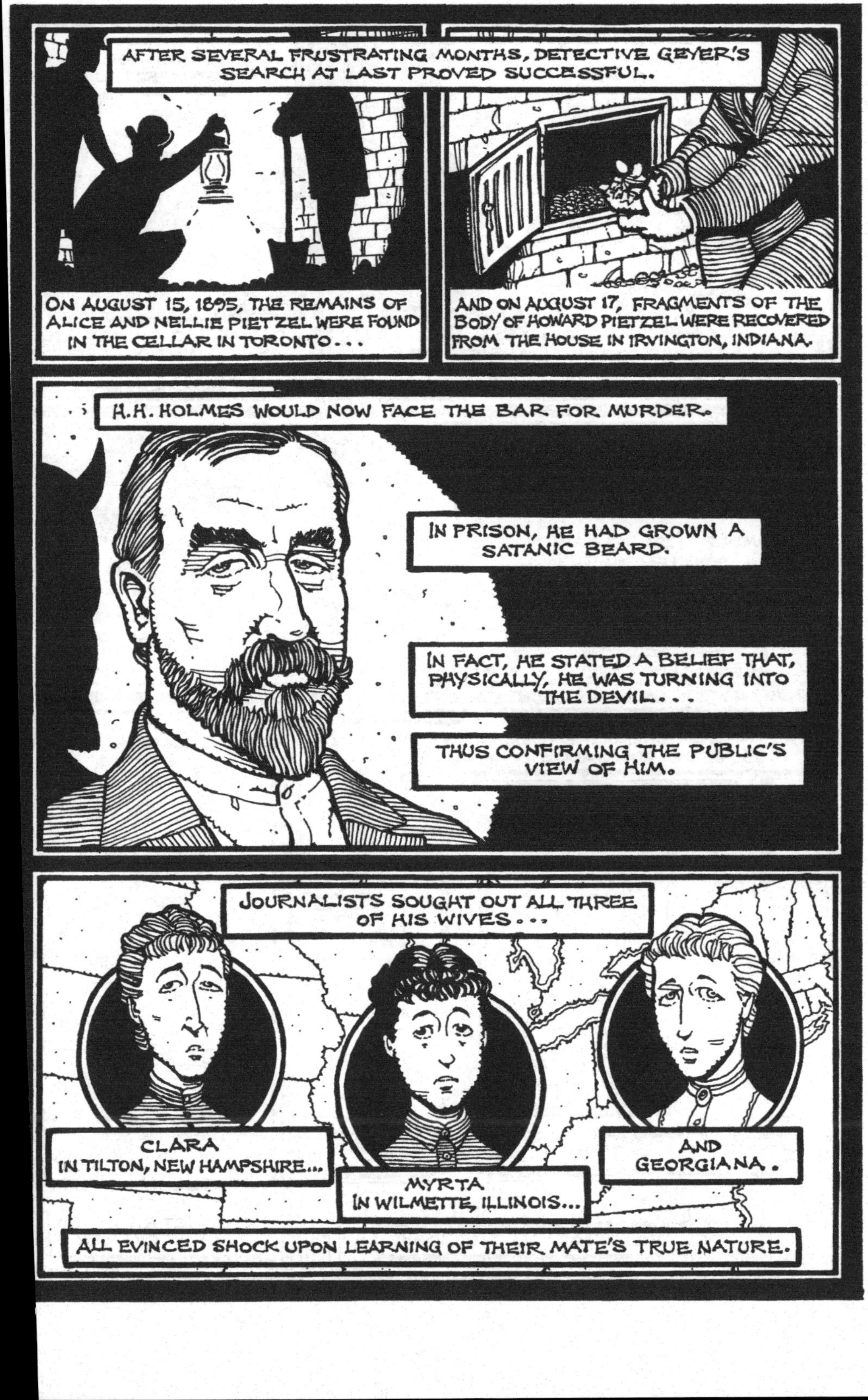
AFTER SEVERAL FRUSTRATING MONTHS, DETECTIVE GEYER'S SEARCH AT LAST PROVED SUCCESSFUL.
ON AUGUST 15, 1895, THE REMAINS OF ALICE AND NELLIE PIETZEL WERE FOUND IN THE CELLAR IN TORONTO . . .
AND ON AUGUST 17, FRAGMENTS OF THE BODY OF HOWARD PIETZEL WERE RECOVERED FROM THE HOUSE IN IRVINGTON, INDIANA.
H.H. HOLMES WOULD NOW FACE THE BAR FOR MURDER.
IN PRISON, HE HAD GROWN A SATANIC BEARD.
IN FACT, HE STATED A BELIEF THAT, PHYSICALLY, HE WAS TURNING INTO THE DEVIL . . .
THUS CONFIRMING THE PUBLIC'S VIEW OF HIM.
JOURNALISTS SOUGHT OUT ALL THREE OF HIS WIVES . . .
CLARA IN TILTON, NEW HAMPSHIRE...
MYRTA IN WILMETTE, ILLINOIS...
AND GEORGIANA.
ALL EVINCED SHOCK UPON LEARNING OF THEIR MATE'S TRUE NATURE.

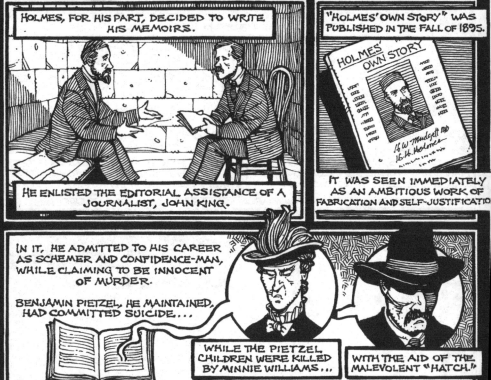

HOLMES, FOR HIS PART, DECIDED TO WRITE HIS MEMOIRS.

HE ENLISTED THE EDITORIAL ASSISTANCE OF A JOURNALIST, JOHN KING.

"HOLMES' OWN STORY" WAS PUBLISHED IN THE FALL OF 1895.

IT WAS SEEN IMMEDIATELY AS AN AMBITIOUS WORK OF FABRICATION AND SELF-JUSTIFICATION.

IN IT, HE ADMITTED TO HIS CAREER AS SCHEMER AND CONFIDENCE-MAN, WHILE CLAIMING TO BE INNOCENT OF MURDER.

BENJAMIN PIETZEL, HE MAINTAINED, HAD COMMITTED SUICIDE...

WHILE THE PIETZEL CHILDREN WERE KILLED BY MINNIE WILLIAMS...

WITH THE AID OF THE MALEVOLENT "HATCH."

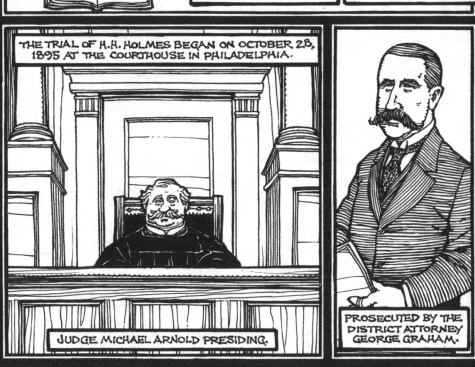

THE TRIAL OF H.H. HOLMES BEGAN ON OCTOBER 28, 1895 AT THE COURTHOUSE IN PHILADELPHIA.

JUDGE MICHAEL ARNOLD PRESIDING.

PROSECUTED BY THE DISTRICT ATTORNEY GEORGE GRAHAM.

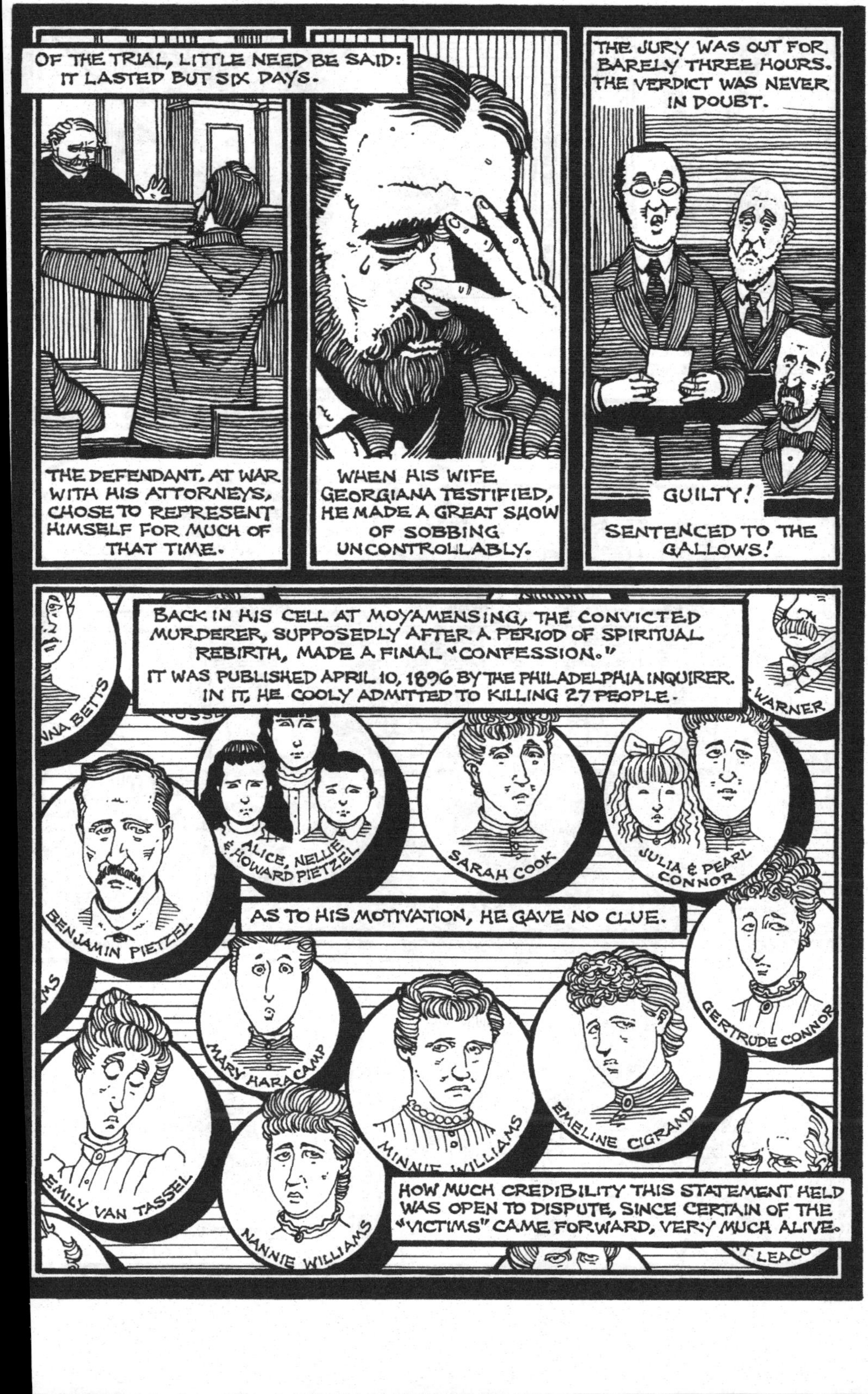
OF THE TRIAL, LITTLE NEED BE SAID: IT LASTED BUT SIX DAYS.
THE DEFENDANT, AT WAR WITH HIS ATTORNEYS, CHOSE TO REPRESENT HIMSELF FOR MUCH OF THAT TIME.
WHEN HIS WIFE GEORGIANA TESTIFIED, HE MADE A GREAT SHOW OF SOBBING UNCONTROLLABLY.
THE JURY WAS OUT FOR BARELY THREE HOURS. THE VERDICT WAS NEVER IN DOUBT.
GUILTY!
SENTENCED TO THE GALLOWS!
BACK IN HIS CELL AT MOYAMENSING, THE CONVICTED MURDERER, SUPPOSEDLY AFTER A PERIOD OF SPIRITUAL REBIRTH, MADE A FINAL "CONFESSION."
IT WAS PUBLISHED APRIL 10, 1896 BY THE PHILADELPHIA INQUIRER. IN IT, HE COOLY ADMITTED TO KILLING 27 PEOPLE.
WARNER
ALICE, NELLIE & HOWARD PIETZEL
SARAH COOK
JULIA & PEARL CONNOR
BENJAMIN PIETZEL
AS TO HIS MOTIVATION, HE GAVE NO CLUE.
GERTRUDE CONNOR
MARY HARACAMP
EMILY VAN TASSEL
EMELINE CIGRAND
NANNIE WILLIAMS
HOW MUCH CREDIBILITY THIS STATEMENT HELD WAS OPEN TO DISPUTE, SINCE CERTAIN OF THE "VICTIMS" CAME FORWARD, VERY MUCH ALIVE.

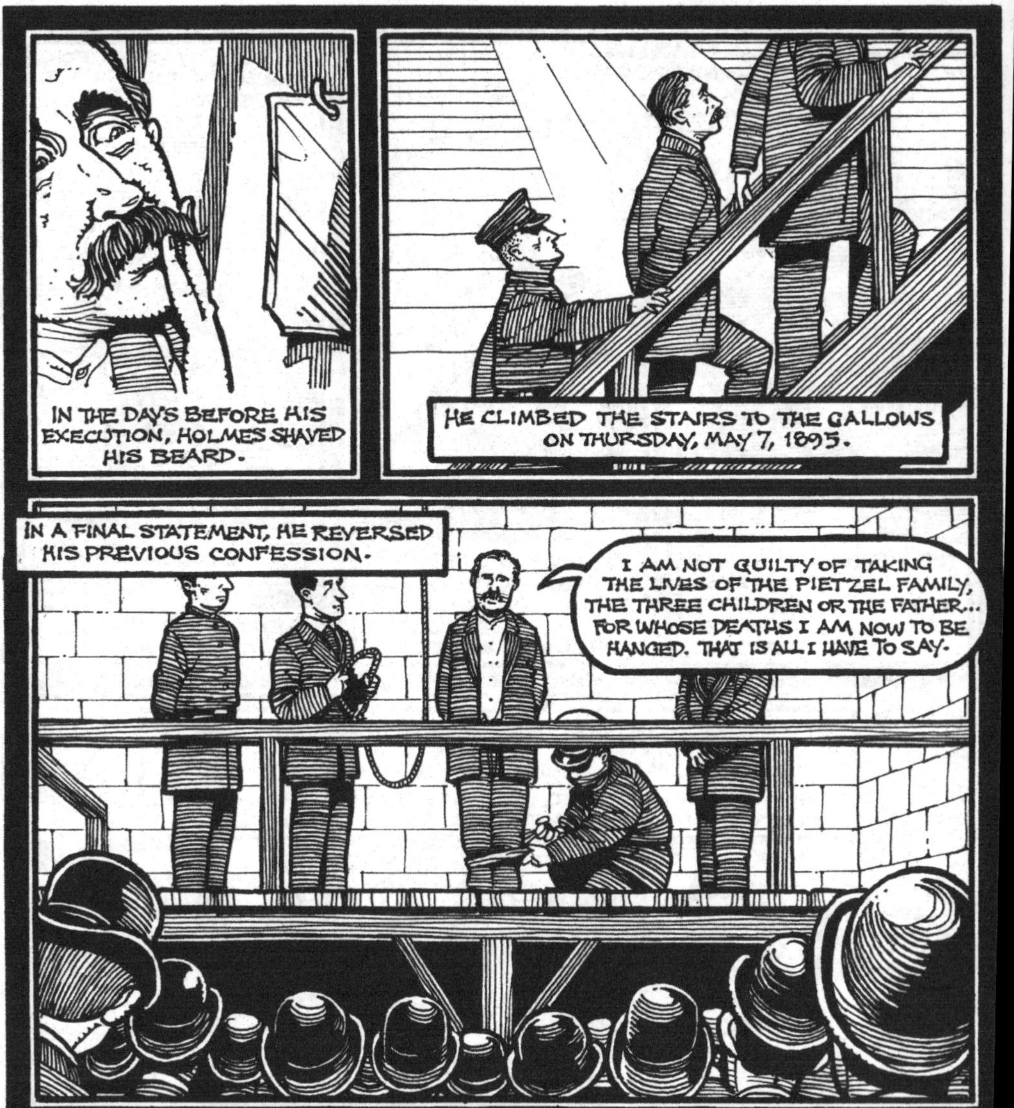
IN THE DAYS BEFORE HIS EXECUTION, HOLMES SHAVED HIS BEARD.
HE CLIMBED THE STAIRS TO THE GALLOWS ON THURSDAY, MAY 7, 1895.
IN A FINAL STATEMENT, HE REVERSED HIS PREVIOUS CONFESSION.
I AM NOT GUILTY OF TAKING THE LIVES OF THE PIETZEL FAMILY, THE THREE CHILDREN OR THE FATHER... FOR WHOSE DEATHS I AM NOW TO BE HANGED. THAT IS ALL I HAVE TO SAY.
THE TRAP WAS SPRUNG AT 10:10 AM.

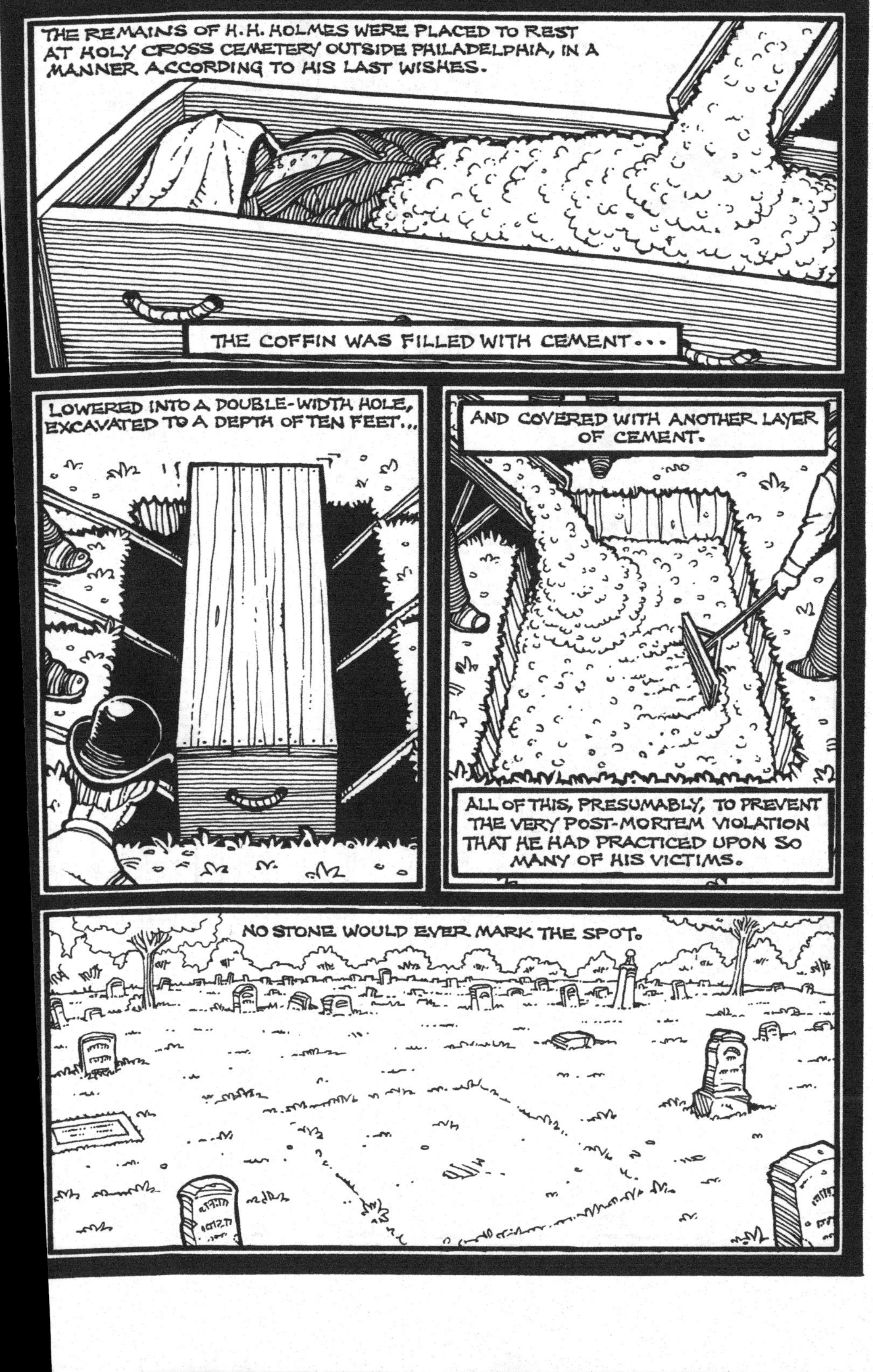
THE REMAINS OF H.H. HOLMES WERE PLACED TO REST AT HOLY CROSS CEMETERY OUTSIDE PHILADELPHIA, IN A MANNER ACCORDING TO HIS LAST WISHES.
THE COFFIN WAS FILLED WITH CEMENT...
LOWERED INTO A DOUBLE-WIDTH HOLE, EXCAVATED TO A DEPTH OF TEN FEET...
AND COVERED WITH ANOTHER LAYER OF CEMENT.
ALL OF THIS, PRESUMABLY, TO PREVENT THE VERY POST-MORTEM VIOLATION THAT HE HAD PRACTICED UPON SO MANY OF HIS VICTIMS.
NO STONE WOULD EVER MARK THE SPOT.

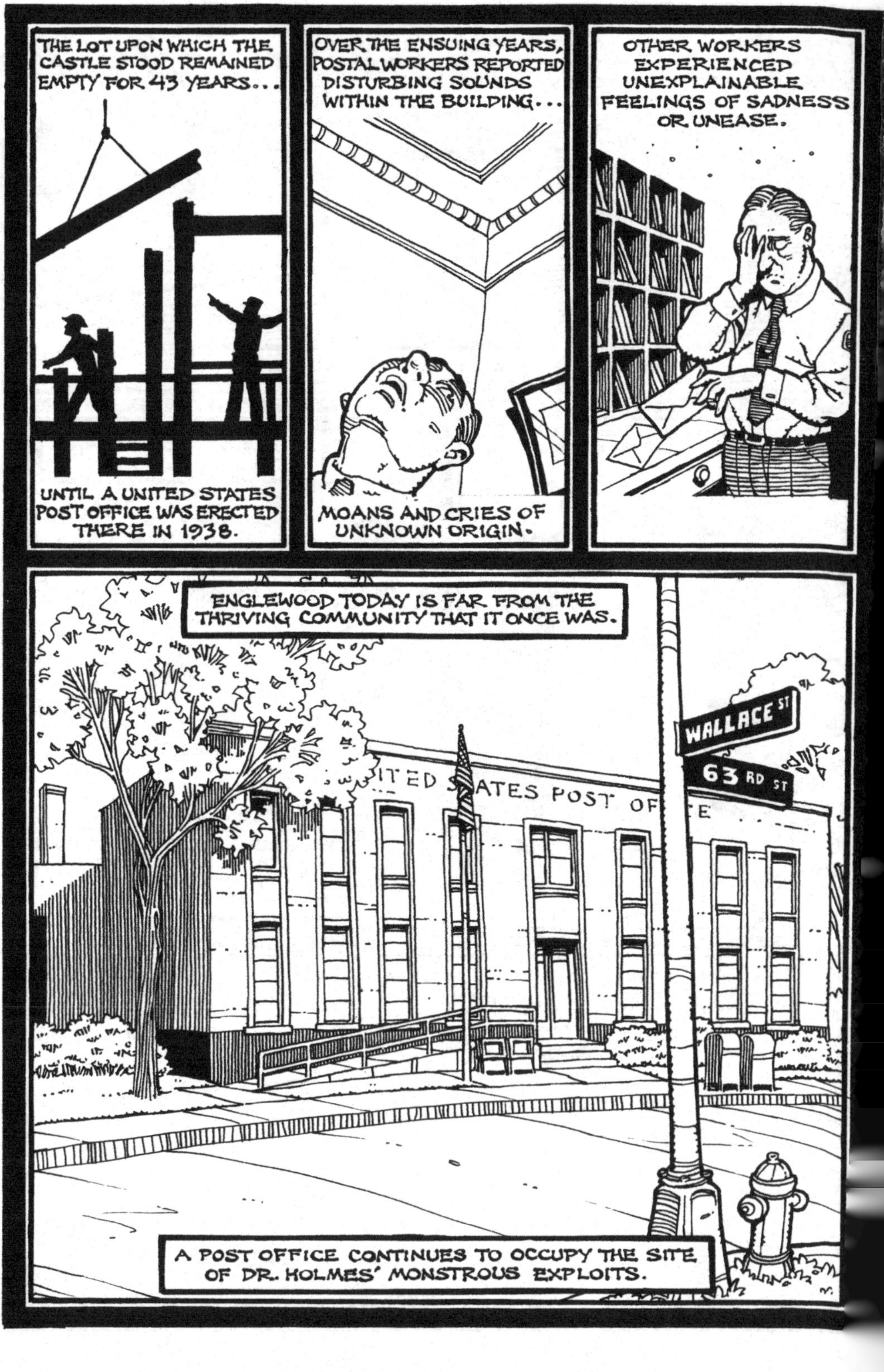
THE LOT UPON WHICH THE CASTLE STOOD REMAINED EMPTY FOR 43 YEARS...
UNTIL A UNITED STATES POST OFFICE WAS ERECTED THERE IN 1938.
OVER THE ENSUING YEARS, POSTAL WORKERS REPORTED DISTURBING SOUNDS WITHIN THE BUILDING...
MOANS AND CRIES OF UNKNOWN ORIGIN.
OTHER WORKERS EXPERIENCED UNEXPLAINABLE FEELINGS OF SADNESS OR UNEASE.
ENGLEWOOD TODAY IS FAR FROM THE THRIVING COMMUNITY THAT IT ONCE WAS.
WALLACE ST
63 RD ST
ITED STATES POST OF E
A POST OFFICE CONTINUES TO OCCUPY THE SITE OF DR. HOLMES' MONSTROUS EXPLOITS.